Monetary Theory: Knapp's Last Speeches

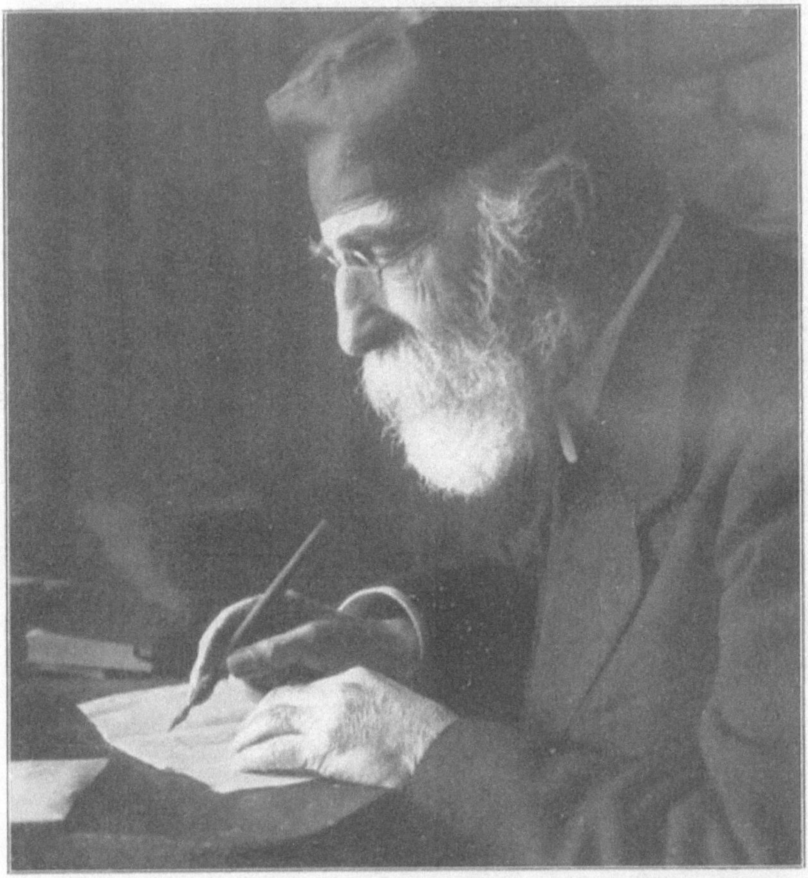

G. F. Knapp

Excerpts translated by Marco Saba from: G.F. Knapp,
Einführung in einige Hauptgebiete der Nationalökonomie
(Introduction to some major fields of economics, 1925)

November 5, 2018

INDEX

Legal historical foundations of the monetary system ………....3

Explanations on the state theory of money ……………….….28

The currency question viewed from the state………………..45

About the theories of the monetary system …………………..61

Austria and the state theory of money………………………..83

Eduard Hammer, a Viennese currency writer ……………....101

The legal historical foundations of the monetary system

Public lecture, held in Stuttgart on April 1906, at the meeting of German historians.

[From Yearbook for Legislation, Administration and Economics, 13d. XXX (1906).)

Content.

The metallic theory of money can not explain all monetary systems, so it is not general enough. The state theory, on the other hand, explains both the "normal" and the "anomalous", for example the Austrian currency. For the unit of value is everywhere a historically - not technically - defined concept created by the legal order,

Money is still the predominant currency in the countries of our culture, but by no means the only one. The payment by weighing metal is already completely overcome; she preceded the use of money and can be passed over here. On the other hand, the giro payment is spreading rapidly and is increasingly replacing the use of money; However, this higher level of payment transactions will not be discussed here either. We limit ourselves to the consideration of money, that is, to the middle of the three mentioned stages, and ask about the legal historical foundations of this institution.

Our states are payment communities and set up rules of law that govern the use of money to make payments. Of course, the citizens, or rather the inhabitants of the state, still have some legitimacy to refuse this or that piece of money under certain circumstances; but it would be a great mistake to believe that such private considerations ultimately govern money use. Non-tacit agreement, not customary law, but governmental orders underlie our monetary constitution. Anyone who defies these commandments encounters the judicial rule of the state and could experience that the state forces him to pay according to the prevailing rules or to make regular payments.

It is a rule of law, for example, that in the German Reich we must pay gold coins indefinitely; that we must accept Taler pieces indefinitely is also a proposition of the law of law, just as it is a rule of law, that we have to take the silver coins with imperial embossing only up to the amount of 20 Marks in payment. Thus we have found the ground upon which to build our views: We have to envisage the legal system of the monetary system.

For the time being let us only hint at the most difficult question in this field: is it a rule of law that our gold coins, which are known to be crowns and double crowns, should read 10 Mk or 20 Mk? It is clear that they are crying so much; But do they do it on the basis of a rule of law or do they do it on the basis of their gold content, that is for technical reasons?

We must reach a decision on this.

In each state, the payments are expressed in units of weight to indicate their size. For us, the unit of value has the name Mark; in France she is called Frank; in England sterling; in Russia rubles. An obligation to pay is known in size when expressed in Germany in Mark; in France, when expressed. in francs.

Furthermore, every state has coins; What the pieces consist of is not important at first; We have coins made of gold, silver, nickel, copper, and certain notes, such as banknotes and Treasury notes (Reichskassenscheine), are still part of these coins. But it is absolutely indispensable that we know how many marks those pieces hold. This validity is determined by the legal system. Very often the validity is stated on the piece. On our gold pieces there is a print of 20 Marks or 10 Marks. But it is not written on our Talers that they count 3 Marks; nevertheless, they are 3 Mk., since this is in our laws. Generally speaking, this means: **The legal system specifies how many value units each coin is valid.**

If a payment is to be made, then, in practical terms, the only question to be asked is: I. how many units of value are to be paid? and 2. How many units of value are the pieces available, as far as they are permissible for that payment?

More than this is not required; The common man, who makes payments or receives payments every day with the help of this little knowledge, does not know any more. If he lives in Germany, he can not offer to offer foreign coins or to accept foreign coins. He knows that our money is a governmental institution, and that the other states, each for themselves, also make their money only for their territory. The pieces are valid only in their area; the validity is thus an institution springing from the legal order; it is based on an order of the state; she is proclamatory. The monetary system always refers to national territories, and if there are states that conclude treaties with their neighbors to make certain types of money common, then such states are no longer independent of each other; in this case, closed treaties create larger areas that must be regarded as a whole. Independent, independent states always have their money only for themselves. One may wish that it would be different; but for legal history it is clear that independent states organize their finances by the state. Therefore, a monetary theory can only be governmental - or dissolve into unhistorical demands.

If we now turn our attention to a particular independent state, no matter which one it is, then the question of the legal historical foundations of finance finally implies the following: In the state the unit of value has a name; its name is Mark; what is the meaning of this name? What is meant by a mark? Is it possible to define the term "mark" in our country, or in France the term "frank"? As long as the value unit is not defined, the theorist remains unsatisfied, so he asks; "What is meant by a mark?" Is the mark about the 1395th part of a pound of fine gold?

But who is meant when I ask, what is meant by a mark? Should there be any information that calls itself an economist? About a teacher at the university or at a commercial college? All right - only I put a condition. Whoever it is, I do not want to hear his private opinion; because otherwise he probably even moves with the paragraph of his book, in which he has pronounced roundly and cleanly, that in his opinion the Mark or the Frank should be this and that; he therefore serves me with a well-considered advice, presumably with a quite excellent one; and instructs me that the dissimilarity is an unfortunate exception; because, unfortunately, it is a curious mood of the state to find institutions that are in conflict with the paragraphs of the professors' book.

But we do not want to be served with advice; The man from whom we expect an answer must first promise us that he examines **the legal order of the state in its historical development, and on the basis of this state of affairs, which for us is the reality**, brings out in a purely observational and reflective manner what the unit of value is. If he has done that, then as an encore we also want to hear patiently what advice for legislation our warden keeps in stock.

So we expect a right-historical answer to our question, which is more precise: what does the state understand by the concept of value unit? For as the state legally orders our payment system, and we are bound by this legal system, we want to hear what the state means. But since he is not a natural person, we can only grasp the answer from his deeds - and the actions of the state are taken from the legal order he has created.

We can refuse our approach and instead propose that older writers and recent college notebooks should be consulted, containing the definition of value unit. But whoever does that does not refute us, unless he refutes our account of the legal constitution of money; because we just want to expose this constitution in its stages of development in order to see what its goals are.

All attacks on the state theory must therefore stand on this ground, on the legal history, or they are mere counter-speech by men who do not want to get involved with the question asked. In other words, this question reads: from what basic idea does the legal system of monetary affairs appear logical? If we prove such a fundamental idea, it is to be recognized as the legal-historical basis of the monetary system, regardless of whether we like it or not.

Let us first hear the prevailing opinion; We want to call their bearers metallists without paying any attention to the fact that there are monometallists and bimetallists.
The metallist explains all appearances by the two keywords metal and credit. He begins first with the sentence: a mark means the 1395th part of a pound of fine gold, because the metal gold is expressed in us in this proportion in 90-Mark pieces boundlessly, what is missing, the melallist explains from the credit.

Let's get involved in this metallistic point of view and look back to the earliest times that the metalist always imagines. The obligation to pay so many units of value, in fact, originally means: someone is to deliver a certain weight of a metal. In it, the metallist is quite right, as everyone admits, because no one claims that the metallist only recounts fantasies.

The question of which metal to deliver, we leave aside, as I said: be it ore, be it silver, be it gold - that's no different to us. All these metals are originally considered only as a substance; development thus begins with autometallism; the term "auto" means the indifference of all form and the materiality of the substance in and of itself.

The next stage of development is so described by the metallists: the metal is formed; weighed pieces of metal are brought into the form of coins and legally approved only in this form when payments are to be made. The metal chosen by the state is infinitely convertible into such coins.
Thus, in the place of the formless means of payment, the

formed - and this formed means of payment is the earliest form of money; it is money.

The bare money is the first type of money that appears in legal history. Our German gold coins, as well as the English and French, are still money today. Before the year 1871 our Taler money was money, because then the silver was infinitely convertible into money - whereas today only the gold has this property. Note that even the boundless negotiability of any metal for cash is a property which is based on the legal system: this order gives the metal this property or withdraws it from it.

But there are other money besides: our silver coins are certainly money, but not cash; as well as our nickel and copper coins; even our paper cash notes are money and the banknotes are money; but they are not hard money, but emergency (nominal) money: they lack the property that the material of which the plates are made is boundless transformable into the money in question.

How does the metalist relate to this phenomenon? He does not deny it, because that would be a tangible limitation. Rather, the metalist says: the emergency money is based on credit; it is credit money; and this means that there must be an institution in the state which allows the owner of the emergency money to receive cash on request; For the metalist, the nominal money consists of instructions for money. And in fact: we can have silver coins, copper coins, nickel coins officially changed into gold money; the Reichsbank, as the central office for the administration of the money, procured this change *ex officio*, likewise it dissolves the Reich treasury notes and the bank notes in "cash".

From this follows: The two keywords metal and credit are at best sufficient to explain our current German monetary constitution; either the money is cash: then it is sufficient to define the unit of value metallistically; or the money is nominal: then it is an instruction on cash money. Other types of money do not occur. So the theory of metallists is enough; One can therefore say that the value unit Mark is now the 1395th part of a pound of fine gold; and in the earlier constitution, before 1871, it was similar: the unit of value, called Taler, was the 30th part of a pound of fine silver.

For it is well known that the pound of gold is now spread at 1395 marks; and earlier, the pound of silver was spread to thirty Talers.
In both cases, the respective value unit is definable as a certain amount of precious metal.

So far the theory of metallists reaches; it is so clear that every child understands it; it even seems self-evident, so much so, that many or all scholars are surprised to hear the name of metallism ringing in it: this, they think, is not one theory among others, but it is simply the theory of money; Surprised they exclaim: we have always been metallists, but what else could they have been! You have also voluntarily admitted that, in case of need, metallism is sufficient to explain our constitution of money; So: why the noise?

But let us only speak. You metallists can explain our monetary condition; our current and our previous one. But these are not special cases. We demand a theory of money for all constitutions. Can you metalists explain all monetary constitutions? - that's the point, and that's not proven yet.

Special solutions prove nothing. It is important to find the general solution of the task.

Maybe there are monetary constitutions that resist the melallistic theory. And indeed, there are such. Then the metalist becomes impatient and exclaims: Such reluctant constitutions are anomalous, they are changed, they are not tolerated, for they are exceptions.

But after all, in spite of all the abnormality, after all, it is money.

It is precisely through their intolerance that the metalists admit that they can not explain all monetary constitutions, but only the "normal ones." This is the weak point in the system of metallists: they must distinguish the real monetary constitutions into normal ones that they can explain, and in abnormal ones, for which they lack the key, for it is no longer true for the abnormal that the value-unit is a certain quantity of metal.

Such abnormal constitutions are indeed present in all states for a time; it suffices to give as an example the Austrian constitution, as it was from 1866 to 1892. Let's take a closer look. It was known as the "Austrian currency", with the word currency being taken in the broader sense, meaning monetary.
According to this, the Austrian state made its payments in non-redeemable banknotes and in non-redeemable government notes. Whoever had to claim 1000 guilders from the state received this amount in banknotes or in national notes; on each of these leaves was an amount called gulden; so many leaves were obtained that the sum totaled was 1000 guilders. When

the banknotes at the bank, the national notes at the central cashier's office of the state, were demanded to demand silver gulden pieces, the cashier shrugged his shoulders or broke into an almost rude laughter: "Do not you know that the banknotes and the State notes are not redeemable? " **So you had paper in your hand, and there could be no doubt that <u>you had no instructions on silver money</u> in the hand.**

The metalist had his two keywords, metal and credit, on his tongue; but with the metal it was certainly nothing; So the other cue had to be: credit. When it comes to legally effective instructions, it makes sense to talk about credit. In Austria, however, such instructions were not mentioned at all. The only thing was just that there is no legally effective instruction there: it is not the banknote, it is not the state note, the various types of coins are also not. What should the metallist begin with?
He made a daring leap and explained briefly and boldly: Credit also takes place when there is no legal redemption in prospect ! So, credit is available even if there is no credit. Credit is just a very strange concept, says the metallist: one can explain the Austrian constitution of the monetary system from the credit - but for the concept of the credit there is still no definition!

By this way out, the metalists have simply admitted that they ran out of breath; but they do not want to admit it and envelop everything with a barrage of words.
How did it look in practice?
Our metallist, with a thousand paper guilders in his hand, says to the cashier: "That's a sheer fraud." The cashier replies, "Do not you know that these paper guilders are compulsory? Pay your creditors with it, the landlord You owe the rent, the tailor

who sent you his bill, and all the other people have to accept the paper. " Our otherwise honest man has only the choice either to continue the fraud suffered to his creditors - or to sit down on a chair and wait until the state and the bank again to redeem in cash, where he fate the Ritter Toggenburg [a ballad by Friedrich Schiller, written in 1797] destiny: "And so he sat, a corpse, one morning there."

At that time there was a monetary constitution in Austria, which, of course, was quite bad because of the foreign trade, but it was sufficient to serve the internal traffic. We are far from recommending her; but it was a money constitution, and that alone is here to be considered.

How was the value unit to be defined then? Was the gulden in which one paid, about the 45th part of a pound of silver? Certainly not; the gulden was not metallistically definable; it was a concept of the legal system, which served only to express the size of the debts and to proclaim the validity of the means of payment.

The connection with the silver was completely eliminated for the guilder, with which one then actually paid. There was a nominal guilder: since 1859, a guilder has been every means of payment which the state declares legally permissible in order to repay a debt, which, however, would have to be redeemed by a silver guilder at the end of 1858.

The unit of value was nominal, and it did not come on the metal content of the means of payment; one could still pay in silver gulden, but one could pay with the same legal effect also in nonredeemable paper gulden. This constitution can not be explained on a metallistic basis, but it is not in itself inexplicable: the unit of value was then nominal; the usual means of payment afforded no real satisfaction in the sense of the metallist; but they granted a circulatory satisfaction under the principle, "Tit for tat."

Do not reply that a nominal unit of value is impossible; That would mean that the constitution of Austria at that time was impossible while it really was. An only nominal unit of value is empirically proven to be possible; Anyone who finds them questionable, who recognizes significant dangers, especially for foreign traffic, must judge that the merely nominal unit of value is indeed possible, but that one is in a hurry to get out of such a state. That is a view that can be heard.

From this follows, as the more insightful metallists suggest, a fork in the theory; instead of one there are two of them; if the monetary condition is good, the value unit can be defined metallistically; By contrast, in this degenerate constitution the value unit is nominal.

But then there is no unified theory; for the two cases exclude each other, it seems; in the first case it is paid by transfer of metal; in the other case, only nominal payments are made; a glaring contrast. So the investigation is over by this twofold solution. There is nothing difficult about it: all divisions are easy to grasp; as long as they present a simple dilemma, such as this: either metal content; or no metal content Applied to our investigation, we would have reached the conclusion: in ordinary states you pay by handing over metal, but in messy states you only pay nominally, that is, without handing over metal.

But if there is a uniform, not twofold, theory of money, then the difficult cases must not be set aside, for that would be a cowardice of theory.

But it must be provable that that dilemma is incorrect. And it is incorrect, as much as this may surprise. The state theory of money can indeed be consistent, because that dilemma is not right.

Nobody believes us on that for the first time. "The only nominal payments in Austria are certainly payments without transfer of metal." I admit. "And the payments in orderly countries like Germany are certainly payments by the transfer of metal, so no nominal payments." I do not admit that.

On the contrary, **I assert that there, as here, every payment, as judged by the state, that is judicially assessed, is a nominal payment.** The difference is just that: in Austria you had nominal payment without transfer of metal, in the German Reich you have nominal payment with transfer of metal.

From a legal point of view, wherever monetary policy is concerned, the nominal payment is the last basis; everywhere the unit of value is nominally defined; but sometimes the pieces you pay for are equipped with metal content, sometimes they are not. The metal content is thus legally not essential for the process of payment. I do not deny the most important and always recognized advantages of the metal content of the pieces, more precisely: the very great importance of the bar constitution, especially for foreign relations.

But being important for economic traffic is something quite different from being essential to the legal system. And in this sense, let it be said: in spite of the constitution of money, the unit of value is nominal; sometimes metal content of the pieces occurs, and sometimes it lacks; The dilemma therefore only opens up when we have recognized the nominality of the unit of value as a common upper characteristic of all monetary constitutions. That is why there can be a simple, common theory of money.

The distinctions, however, are a little finer than one might expect: it all depends on a two-story scheme that is not immediately grasped by one-story spirits. But it is not difficult.

The highest term is the payment. Now, first, ask yourself: is payment made by adding metal? If so, then you have a compensatory payment and the money is still missing. But if the payment is made by handing over drawn pieces, which are proclamatory, then the monetary constitution is there.

Here's the point that the metallists overlooked. They think the money is defined by the metal content; but the metal content is a technical fact. We, on the other hand, give the money a legal definition: drawn pieces with proclamatory validity are money, regardless of whether they have metal content or not. For this we need a short expression: the money is a monetary currency; only the chartality creates money. Means of payment is the further term; as long as there is still consideration, you have no money; the money comes only with the chartality, which is a legal circumstance. This is the first floor of our distinctions.

The second floor looks like this: The money has either cash status or emergency status. Both species are held together by the clause of proclamatory validity: but they are separated by the rules of law concerning the origin. Cash money requires a meta-asset. which can be transformed into coins without limit. Nominal money does not have this requirement.

In such a two-story division, we have the advantage that all monetary constitutions are uniformly encompassed; both the ordinary and the disorderly ones; both the German monetary constitution and the much-vilified Austrian. Then there is, and only then is there a unified theory of money that is known to be lacking in the metallist; but she is not missing us!

Now it is easy to give information about the legal historical foundations of the financial system. Not that the metallists' theory is completely untrue - it's just not the whole truth.

First of all, let's see what the metals really mean. Above all, the earliest stage of payment is autometallistic, that is, tied to the use of a metal.
Second, of course, the technical invention of coinage is also tied to the use of a metal: these are already two quite undeniable services that the metal has done historically. But it is a mistake to say that everything is said here, as the metallists believe. Because the state is still missing with its legal intervention.

The state in its administration of justice creates the purely legal concept of the unit of value; he says: her name is Mark; and he defines the mark by connecting to the former unit of value: the mark is the third part of a Taler. So it is with us; In Austria, the state creates the value unit crown, and defines it by connecting it to the former value unit gulden: the crown is a half gulden. This creates a chain of definitions whose first link is related to autometallism.

Our present units of value are not defined by a quantity of metal, but only the first link in the historical chain of definitions is defined by a quantity of metal. The later terms are only historical and not technically defined. That is the content of the state theory of money.

Accordingly, one can never throw the metal out of the legal history of the monetary system. But you can throw the metal out of the monetary system, but you do not need to do that. You can only do it, but for the time being you're better off keeping the metal. The state theory does not fight the metal use, but it fights only the usual reason of the metal use.

The metallists have too narrow a theory; a genuinely general theory has room for metal use, but does not bind itself to it. But too narrow a theory is always wrong, not because it contains nothing right; but because it does not quite contain the right thing.

The legal historical foundations of the monetary system thus remain incomplete, as long as one speaks only of the technical use of metals; The foundations are only completely perfected when the position of the state and its legal system are taken with equal care. Without the jurisprudence of the monetary system there is no sufficient theory of this phenomenon.

Historians are right in turning their research into coinage. Coin cabinets will always be of great importance, for example because of their insights into the spread of weight systems from Babylonia to the countries of the Mediterranean. But nothing whatsoever is learned about the constitution of money as long as the legal rules for the use of those pieces remain unexplained.

Above all, it has to be investigated: from what time on are the coins proclamatory despite the wear that has occurred?

Only then are they money; only from then on they have a constitution of the Charter; but as long as the actual weight decides, the coins are not money, but pensatory means of payment.

There is some hope for a history of finance, but only if our researchers first of all study the newer monetary constitutions juridically, since only the newer times lie before us in bright and complete illumination. One must first know to what end the monetary constitutions have come in the modern age; otherwise, the precursors of antiquity remain completely incomprehensible.

It is not true that today's education is made clear by the timid approaches of the old days; but the groping attempts of the old days are explained only by the insight into the legal constitution of today's monetary system. Therefore, the state theory of money is also the key to the legal history of payments, while coin history alone can only ever deliver fragments.

However, the theory of the state also teaches modern times to be judged quite differently than has hitherto been customary. "Cash is the main thing; nominal money may only be admitted as a secondary issue, for example for very small payments, whereby it may then appear as a divorce allowance, ie with limited acceptance."

This addiction to bullion, combined with not so much aversion, has been widespread in Germany since 1857 and is considered to be the only one true, as the sound theory.- But what does real development teach us, both in Germany and in England, France, and Austria? It teaches us quite the opposite, namely, that the notable forms of money gain new distribution in every new act of legislation, and for all major payments, we use banknotes and Reich cash notes, but gold pieces only incidentally, and when it is said that these notes are redeemable, I ask, first, who Remember to demand the redemption of the bills?

And secondly, who thinks that the redeeming coffers will also offer Talers, because they are allowed to do so according to our legislation, although the practice does not make use of it; but the Taler since 1871 is nominal money.

It is very similar in our neighboring countries.

So it is true, when we say: in internal traffic, the necessary money prevails in a way that is quite unmistakable. Nominal money types are therefore probably sufficient for internal traffic.

There are even metallists who open themselves to this truth. So the much narrower sentence remains: our cash money has its main use in relations with foreign countries.

Our cash money is known to be gold money; as well as the cash money in England, in France, in Austria. If it essentially serves foreign traffic, as we have seen, then this golden cash is perhaps the long-awaited world money, the money for the much praised world traffic. If so, then a high level of development would have been achieved. But is that the case?

World money is nothing more than a figurative phrase. There

are facilities for world traffic, but the fact that the gold coins of these states are world money is not true. Never was the sentence made more stringent than it is today, that in every state only domestic money is used for payments. The German twenty mark piece does not apply in France. The French twenty Frank is not valid in Germany. There is no world money.

The expansion of the gold standard since 1871 means something very different: the states have chosen the same metal for their cash, namely gold. Our cash money is technically convertible into French cash money; but without this transformation, it does not apply there.

The purpose of this measure is to maintain a firm course between German and French money; the Frank is to cost 81 pfennigs, if the German wants to buy Franks on the stock exchange. This institution is excellent - but who can be so non-juristic to speak of world money here? It just orders a currency hike, and that's something else.

Accordingly, our cash money is used primarily for fixing the exchange rates. If there were other means for this purpose, then the cash money would not be so important even in foreign traffic - but we would rather avoid the prospect of such possibilities.

Let's stick with the development that has now been achieved: emergency money in internal traffic; cash, golden, because of foreign traffic. This is the meaning of the gold currency introduced almost everywhere today. So let's hold on!

It took me long enough to get there. But do not think that blessing is based on gold. With silver as the metal for our cash, we could have achieved the same thing; but England had gold, and the other states joined.

Let's summarize everything briefly said.

All men more easily comprehend the phenomena of the sensible world than the spiritual world; All laymen understand the inventions of technology more easily than the inventions of legal life. Trailed cannons and smokeless powder are more understandable than the organization of the army. Thus, in the constitution of the payment system, too, the sensual part is far more comprehensible than the administrative part.

Everybody understands the autometallism that we no longer have; but few understand the constitution of the money we have, for it is based on laws governing the use of the pieces, and on an administrative activity that keeps the international course in order.

The legal system is always formalistic, which is why the state theory of money is fundamentally quite formalistic. Anyone who wants to understand the monetary system must put himself on the ground of legal life, and then the question is no longer whether one wants to think in a formalistic way or not - but then formalistic thinking is a necessity.

The task of the theorist is thus posed: from which basic idea does the legal system of monetary affairs appear internally consistent? To find this basic idea is the matter of the analytical mind. We find it in the sentence often mentioned: the unit of value is nominal, it is a historical concept, and it has no technical content *per se*. Those who do not like this result must either prove that we are wrong in the development of the basic idea; or he must say: such a legal system should not exist. But then he must propose a different legal system and ensure that it is realized.

So far, it has not been experienced that individual know-it-all are rewriting the legal order; for it is based on a historical becoming whose goals are not predicted from the outset, but only later are these goals recognized by the theoretician after the unconsciously acting practice has created a fact.

And so it is quite clear today: the monetary system is supported by inventions of technology in its becoming, but it is not a spawn of technology, but a creature of law. The legal system, however, is not finished from the outset; it gradually emerges from fragments offered by the practitioners - every historian knows that - and only later will the legal historians trace this back to their basic ideas. To do this for the field of finance is the goal of the state theory of money.

From the report by B. Hilliger on the course of the second day of the ninth assembly of German historians, Stuttgart, May 17 to 21, 1906, we insert the following passage here: (Historische Vierteljahrschrift 1906, No. 9, page 297)

The evening of this day also brought a public lecture on "The Legal Historical Foundations of Finance" by the Strasbourg political economist Professor Dr. Georg Friedrich Knapp His remarks were directed against the opinion of the metallists, who tried to explain our whole monetary system with the two key words metal and credit.

Their theory fails because of the phenomena of the present and the experiences of the recent past. Such an abnormal monetary constitution as the Austrian currency from 1866 to 1892 scoffs at the classification into this system.

But can a theory be considered correct, where the exception with the rule fight? No, you have to reconcile both. The theory of metallists is too narrow, it is not completely true. The metal is not the decisive factor; which one ascribes to him for the currency, because each payment would remain a nominal payment, which in Germany with delivery of metal, in Austria of that time however without such a one played.

Decisive for the order of the monetary system in all cases would be the legal status, which lends him the state, because he determines the validity, which is to have the single coin. Thus, money itself remains only a creature of law.

The speech of Knapp was a witty contemplation, recounted with the admirable rhetoric of a great virtuoso whom one liked to listen to, also because it was riddled with innumerable great and small malice against all other people who did not agree with him.

The tendency that carried it was perhaps even deeper than it was expressed in his words. Just as a historical anecdote, even if it is not true, occasionally sheds light on a situation or a person, here too, whether true or false, a word was narrated that the speaker had last expressed himself in a narrower circle that coin collecting had one more level lower than collecting stamps. All the more can one complain that such an interesting and important issue was settled in a public lecture that did not allow the opponents to speak.

For there would probably have been a lively debate that would have been instructive and encouraging for both parties. However, on the other day, a meeting of the Conference of State Historical Publishing Institutes, where the director of the Royal Coin Collection in Berlin, Professor Dr. Menadier, who took the opportunity to test the new theory for its sufficiency, and to show that Knapp's alleged omnipotence of the state did not exist for the order of money in long periods of historical development.

At the places mentioned, Issue 3, page 633, the following reply:

Coinage and money.

In the *Historisches Vierteljahrschrift* of 1906, Issue 2 (page 994 ff.) there is an excellent report on the Ninth Assembly of German Historians, which also discusses a lecture I have given on "the legal-historical foundations of the monetary system."

It is quite true that I have declared mercilessly: money can not be explained by coinage, but nothing is further from a reduction in the study of coinage, for the very reason that suffices for me, because I am not at all privy to studying coinage and, in my very nature, the least disparaging of sciences I do not practice, so I ask you to explain a little the words above, which I certainly maintain. It is the meaning of the term "money."

Money is our predominant means of payment, but not the only thing that occurs in history, which explains why the word money is used by the public in the sense of the means of payment.

For me, the word money has a much narrower meaning, because for me it is a legal - not a technical - term. The money for me is given only when movable things, which are accurately described by the legal system according to substance and form - especially after the signs that carry them - are equipped with "proclamatory" validity in units of value, it follows, firstly, that I have to count irrefutable notes (as they occur in Austria) safely to the money, in which I remain in harmony with the usage of language, which speaks of "paper money": such notes are in Austria so many guldens (now crowns); and the gulden, or the crown is the Austrian value unit.

Secondly, however, it follows that I must not count all trade coins for money; in Austria, ducats shaped by the emperor are no money; Neither do the Maria Theresa Talers, which were coined by the Emperor: for, as is well known, these proclaimed pieces lack the proclamatory validity of units of value; they do not "apply", although they have value as things, according to the known fluctuating market prices in gulden.

From the proclamation of the pieces, however, all the phenomena of the newer monetary system follow without exception: the exchange rates with their fluctuations, the so-called changes in the value of the two noble metals, the occasional agio of certain types of money, the transition from one currency to another - louder things, on which I gave a detailed account in the "State Theory of Money", Leipzig 1905.

But it is easy to see that the proclamatory validity of the pieces is not a technical but a legal characteristic.

Therefore, this side of the financial system, which I consider to be the main thing, can not be studied on the collectibles of a coin cabinet; To put it bluntly, this means that the monetary system can not be recognized from the study of coins.

For the monetary system reaches beyond the coinage, because of the money-equipped bills; and as far as coins are present in the system of money-types of a country, the coin-researcher would be able to ascertain only subordinate characteristics of these pieces, since **the legal position of the pieces** does not fall within the range of its investigations.

Therefore, both areas of research are separate; but I have neither said nor meant that enmity should prevail between them.

Strasbourg i. E., June 26, 1906.
G. F. Knapp.

Explanations on the State Theory of Money
[From Yearbook for Legislation, Administration and Economics, Vol. XXX (906).]

Content.

The so-called "good with fixed value" - the so-called "purchasing power of money". - The nature of the assignats danger. - The real trouble with unredeemable paper money. - The crookedness of the criticism. - Postscript about W. Lexis.

The "state theory" of money asserts that the unit of value is always nominal, that is, that it is an only historically defined term that traffic and the law apply to express the size of payments. The use of metal for the production of means of payment is by no means excluded and even has significant advantages, especially at the beginning of historical development; but the value unit must not be defined as metal quantity. Whoever defines it that way is called a metallist.

Thus, the nominalists differ from the metallists only in the field of definition; it is by no means the practical question of whether or not the means of payment should be made of metal. No sooner was the nominalist conception than for the first time rigorously carried out, did the metallists raise the most vivid contradiction; they argued that there must be a good of immutable value, such as one or the other of noble metals; This good was a measure of value and it had to be, so that the payments could get started.

This "fundamental theory" has completely overlooked this quite fundamental proposition, and for that very reason it should be rejected, though otherwise it would contain all kinds of bad remarks that could serve to improve conventional teaching.

It would be strange, however, if the "State Theory" were so forgetful, but there can be no question of it. "What the metallists perceived as a gap, they themselves could easily have filled out, since they did not do it, we help a little.

The metalist can not do otherwise; he must entertain the view that a certain good is a value-meter; for this assertion is fundamentally the same as the other proposition: the unit of value is a definite set of a good, such as a metal; A third sentence also belongs here: whoever defines price as the quantity of metal which one must give to buy a commodity, he also says the same thing, namely: that that metal is a value meter. The intertwining of these three propositions is logical from the standpoint of metallism.

But if the nominalists do not say all this, it is not an accidental omission, but they simply deny that those propositions are correct - correct in the sense of the universal truth - and have no reason to be in such half-sentences. Semi-true sentences arise from unsuccessful formulation, whereby something accidental is considered essential.

Let us examine, when a commodity exists, of which a certain quantity has a fixed price in units of value (mark, guilder, Frank, etc.). Suppose that there is such a good, then it is understood by most people as a measure of value. But in which cases does this phenomenon occur?

There are two such cases and nothing more.

First case: if ore, silver or gold is treated as a means of payment in itself, ie in the autometallistischen constitution, then the metal in question is such a good. The metalist now says that since silver (or gold) was a commodity of immutable value, it was introduced as a means of payment. But nominalists say that since they had decided at that time to use silver (or gold) as a means of payment, metal by definition had its fixed price and appeared as a value meter. For, in our opinion, the use of that good as a means of payment is to blame for appearing as a good of fixed value. But being a means of payment is a legal term. All the goods - not the one - that the state would have treated as it treated silver or ore in the lines of autometallism, would have exhibited the quality of immutable value and appeared to the laity as a measure of value. "This or that good is a measure of value" means here quite simply: it is explained in itself as a means of payment.

The search for a good of immutable value, or the expectation that such a thing will ever be found, belongs to the frequent confusion of the technical world with the juridical; one expects of nature a phenomenon that can only occur in the spiritual life. But let us not forget that we do not pay with well-balanced metal; Autometallism is long gone.

The second case is much more important: in some countries, which already have a cash flow chart, that is to say, some metal has a fixed price (for example, gold for us, with one pound, with very little variation, 1395 marks). Is gold here, then, the measurer? It seems to the layman. But with balanced gold we are not paid. The fixed price arises with us quite differently than in the case previously considered, namely, in that the state artificially regulates the price of gold; he pays 1392 marks for every pound; and he makes sure that in valuta money (here in the gold coins) one pound of gold is found for every 1395 marks.

The fixed price of gold is thus a consequence of existing institutions: the value of the gold is fixed *ex institutione*. As long as this device exists, the gold may appear to the layman as a measure of value; but if the decor ceased, that would not change the validity of our pieces. So in reality it is very different from what the layman believes: the nominal unit of value is our measure of value.

Other than these two cases are unknown to me; in both cases, however, a property which belongs to the means of payment as such is erroneously transferred to a natural cause.
So the nominalist needs not to talk about a good, which is a value meter.

The metalist, on the other hand, unconsciously imagines the matter as follows: anyone who demands a price for his grain compares first with a metal; He decides to demand as many units of weight as possible, and now calculates the number of units of value (mark, guilder) using the coin's foot.

But we say: the seller immediately mentions the number of florins, crowns, etc., and as a rule does not know the coin's foot; because he thinks of the means of payment only on what he can buy in turn tomorrow.

How long will - in our textbooks - gold still remain a value meter? How long will our teachers still wait for the good of immutable values? Until the legal nature of the concept of payment is understood. -

A similar tangle of misunderstandings exists in the phrases of the purchasing power of money, the value of money, and the rise in prices in the so-called deterioration of money.

The disentanglement of these ideas succeeds only if the position of money within the state is strictly distinguished from the relations of our money to that of the neighboring states.

Suppose, for example, that in Austria, after 1859, irredeemable paper money came into valuta status, and that the exchange rate course against Germany was unfavorable for Austria. The Austrian silver gulden have an *agio*, because it is technically convertible into German Taler pieces.

In this case, says the metallist, everyone sees that the value of Austrian valuta money (namely, the irrecoverable banknotes) is lower than before; the Austrian money has lost in purchasing power; most likely in Austria, the prices of all goods must rise. If we start with the prices, the metallists say that the price means a quantity of metal; From this point of view, it is not illogical to suppose that now all prices must rise; because for a paper guilder is now less silver to buy than before.

Obviously, this is the reason why Metallist considers a general rise in prices in the interior of the country, for example in Austria, to be likely.

But what does the observation of reality say? Here it is to be distinguished, whether one speaks of prices, which were already arranged, when the insoluble paper money became valuta, or whether it concerns prices from developing new purchase transactions.

In the first case we take as an example: I recently sold my house, and today the price of 100,000 guilders is to be paid; In the meantime, however, the irreconcilable paper money has become valuta and fallen in the course against Germany. Do I now have to demand more than 100,000 guilders in paper? No! No judge helps me to obtain more than the 100,000 guilders previously agreed; I have to settle for the nominal payment of that sum, paid in paper. Such prices do not change, because they are from the outset nominal prices.

In the second case, these are newly completed purchases. I sell my house only now, after the unredeemable paper money has become valuta. Will I charge more than 100 000 gulden for this? Maybe, because I will, however, strive for greater proceeds; but will I enforce it? That depends on the balance of power between me and the buyers and thus remains indefinite; on the other hand, it is certain that the changes in the monetary system will have no effect whatsoever; because even these prices do not mean metal quantities, but nominal amounts.

The notion that the "deterioration" of money has the effect of raising prices within the country is thus not factual: it is only an inference from the mistaken view of the metallists about the nature of the price. This is how the metallists use it - the value of valuta money (in this case of indissoluble banknotes) has nevertheless fallen against the silver, as we see in the agony of the silver gulden.
This is undoubtedly true; but it is without legal significance;

By comparing the metalist to the silver, he does something permissible, but when he thinks that something legal follows, he avails himself of private jurisprudence, which the state coldly ignores. The state does not permit any legal implications of that fact; so the courts of the state do not do it; And so the "traffic" must submit, and even if one maintains that the merchants would then reject the money as not good enough, then the merchant is badly known, for he prefers poor payment rather than none at all.

The metallists' efforts to use the metal for comparison are only unconscious wishes regarding the reintroduction of cash. Inside the state, because of the balance of power between demand and supply, all prices are constantly changing; but they do not do it because of alleged changes in the value of money, because inside one can only say: valuta money presents the value, it is the tangible thing whose transmission legally means the transmission of values; but there is no good at the price of which the state judges whether the money is still as effective as before; the money remains legally always the same effect, it "applies" proclamatory.

How much of this or that good - even a metal - you can buy for it, the state is indifferent.

The "purchasing power" of money within the state is nothing other than the reciprocal consideration of prices, that is, it changes only in so far as prices change, depending on power relations, there is a general diminution of the purchasing power of money, or a general increase in purchasing power that is just as little as there is a general increase or decrease in prices: Money as such does not buy, any more than the dagger as such kills. The demand that money always preserve its purchasing power is a logical absurdity, for it means that in all purchase transactions the balance of power of the parties should remain unchanged!

But the inter-valutary price, the metalist argues, shows the changed purchasing power of money; If the guilder drops on the stock exchange in comparison to the Taler, then it has diminished purchasing power.

This too is a tautology; diminished purchasing power means quite the same thing as sinking the rate of gulden against the German Taler - so can not explain this sinking.
However, a sinking or rising of the guilder against the Taler has no effect on the gulden in Austria, because this is a juridical phenomenon, whereas on the stock exchange, where guldens are "traded" for Taler, the foreign money as merely a commodity comes into consideration.

The change in the rate of exchange of exchange rates is thus a mercantile phenomenon, from which, as has been said, no inference is allowed on the behavior of money within the state.

These things are strictly different.

Therefore, phrases such as the value of money and the purchasing power of money are fatal to theoretical treatment, because they result from insufficient separation of internal affairs and relations with other countries; So who works with those expressions helps to confuse what has just been unraveled with difficulty.

So you talk about changing prices of the metal in the interior of the country; Let us also speak of a change in the behavior of local valuta money over the foreign one; but do not bring everything clear back into the dark by talking so indefinitely about the "value of money" or the "purchasing power of money," teaching the reader the idea that money is equally distributed in terms of both uses could be of varying effectiveness, that is, as it were, a being of variable condition.

The metallists should be grateful if they are offered clear notions instead of complaining about enrichment! And if some older expressions are dropped because of their darkness, it is all the more appreciated.

It is completely unjustified, however, to demand from the theory of the state that all ideas should be contained in it, for the abolition of which it is actually brought to life! If, in the process, the value of the so-called doctrine of the one or the other old-fashioned sentence should fail, then it is no harm. For there is no theory in which one speaks, without choice and without clearness, of terms which are as general as possible, but where, on the basis of given historical facts, one develops the necessary basic ideas necessary for understanding.

What is dispensable, that can be dispensed with at all, The "state theory" is based essentially on the recent education of the payment system and therefore also considered among other things, the insoluble paper money - without suggestions. At the reader grasps the fear, as if would be encouraged to Assignats economy. How can one be so frightened ! We only spoke of phenomena that can not be denied out of history, and which must therefore be explained.

It is quite expressly to say here, however, what has perhaps been underestimated as self-evident: should the state suddenly apply the coin which, for example, has been considered to have been ten francs, and with this validity issued by it to the state? To diminish validity so that it is accepted by the state at only 5 francs or even lower - this is a process that the "state theory" does not defend itself.

The state - that theory assumes - is intended to uphold all existing debts and treat all means of payment in all their uses equally, be it by giving or taking them.
If the state does not make payments to which it has committed itself, and if it accepts certain means of payment less than what it spends, it undermines the legal system for which it is called.

If, therefore, new masses of irredeemable paper money were created by the state without interruption and later refused to be fully accepted by the public purse - these are the abuses that are not even mentioned by the "state theory" - let alone recommended it, since we did not have to look at lottery management, but at ordered states to describe the recent development of law.

Now suppose that the state adheres to this rule, so he accepts the pieces to the same extent as he gives them, which was always the case, for example, in the times of the Austrian currency. On the other hand, in order to stand by this example, the state is forced to issue irrecoverable cash notes ("state notes"), which is known to have happened from May 1866 to December 1867: the amount of such notes rose to 319 million guilders. Where is the fatality of this event, which is so ruthlessly condemned by all sides?

First of all, it must be stated that a state which can not help itself otherwise acts suicidal if it does not apply this procedure in its greatest need. The objections of the economists are then thought of quite unpolitically and are rightly ignored. But we want to regard this as conceded and only investigate where the evil is located.

At least not in internal payments; As noted above, the general confusion of all prices is out of the question. Only the metal that previously served to create cash (in our sense of the word) is affected in its pricing, which is not a national misfortune. In most cases, however, there is a strong disruption of the inter-valutary rates, for example the German-Austrian exchange rate. That is certainly a great evil. But to avert it, by no means must that paper money be removed from the world; it is sufficient that the state secures the possession of so much foreign means of payment, that it can act as overpowering speculator in currency on the stock exchange in order to keep the course at a certain height. Then this evil has been removed from the world.

The one great malady in the era of the Austrian currency was thus the want of an exodromic administration-and this defect no longer exists; the inter-valutary courses are firm because they are now fixed.

Nevertheless, there is still something unexplained left. Those 312 million gulden in paper are as it were out of nothing, as by magic; so they will not be wealth but dizziness; But the metallists do not want the frauds, and they are quite right. But

who said that the 312 million gulden in state notes were a good in the natural sense of the word? We certainly do not. They represent an administrative remedy for internal payments; these payments are only mutual settlements. The seller of grain is thereby enabled to pay for his clothes and shoes.
Such processes continue to occur even when using means of payment whose natural value is zero, because the legal validity is independent of the value of the plates.

It is the great error of the metallists that they regard this state, which they may fight as abnormal, as anomalous, that is, as if no proper payment were made.

Not in the payment system, but in the financial administration of the state, the consequences of the magic agent come to light. The state as an economic person has certain consequences, because nothing becomes nothing. So a very different area has to be touched here.

In his coffers, the state then only finds paper whose use inside is possible; but these means of payment allow no natural use; they only have legal qualities.

Cash money, on the other hand, would have the same legal and natural properties. This is a huge difference, least denied by those who seek to clarify all this.

Now there is always the fear that the state will exaggerate dangerous magic; he does that sometimes, but only when it is about being or non-being. We think of a state which, by means of regular estimates, considers its expenses beforehand, and therefore has an overview of the necessary revenues; He intends to procure these revenues through taxes, business acquisitions, loans, and the like, but not by issuing government notes, of which he already has enough, as in Austria.

Then the state has put the artificial means of payment in place of the natural; he has a payment transaction, but he does not have the advantages that can be achieved by cash on the side; that is, apart from the internal payment system; in the loss of these advantages lies the deteriorated position of the state.

Those state notes are only means of payment and nothing more; if you abolish them and burn the leaves, you get nothing for the ashes.

If cash had existed on its own, and had it been abolished as a means of payment, then the amount of metal won by melting could have been sold.

So: from nothing you can make legally effective means of payment; but when they die legally, no natural good remains in the hands of the state, for such goods are not created by the will of the state.

If the state is completely devoid of stocks of foreign currency or stocks of metal that can be converted into foreign currency, it can not regulate the exchange rate against foreign countries. Hence, more recently, the accumulation of gold reserves, through metal picking or gold bonds.

But if such aids are available, the course can be fixed against foreign countries, which otherwise would remain completely unregulated.

Then the state still has the disadvantage of not having any salable material in the abolition of the national notes; but nobody will claim that the internal or external payments are in disorder.

However, nothing is suggested here! Let us consider that a theoretician must certainly give priority to the most instructive cases, that is to say, those which appear to the laity most dubious. From this arise for the listener all sorts of side-tones, which have a certain oratorical effect; he always means what should be explained, is also recommended!

May I add a comment on the criticism under which the "state theory" suffers?

It comes thereby a conflict of the basic concept. It is customary to arrange theoretical economics in such a way that it promotes the attainment of certain aims by means of general propositions; It is therefore in the service of the oughts.
On the other hand, the "state theory" wants to describe a legal development of the law and to say what its basic idea is, ie it is in the service of being - as a witty man has expressed by letter (Max Weber).

Have the critics paid enough attention to this? It does not seem to me; they did not even know what they were about to do, not even those who, with the utmost honesty, emphasized all the right details.
Not to mention the abundance of misunderstandings that came from not fully observing terminology. These are the following: According to recent developments, payment is no longer a process that takes place between two persons by the surrender

of a good (in the natural sense of the word). There are number communities, of which the state is the most important. Within the numerical communities, the legal-historical concept of value unit is created.

The central leadership of the Community decrees that certain movable things be understood as carriers of value units. The transfer of such things, that is the money, causes payment. Such an order of payment traffic is, of course, limited to the perimeter of that community, especially the state.

For inter-state transport, special facilities must be added to establish a fixed level of the inter-party rate.
All this has evolved from the circumstance that the judge created the nominality of the unit of value, gradually, almost unconsciously; which nominal noun is compatible with metal pieces, for their validity is proclamatory as well.

Within this framework countless monetary constitutions are possible; nowhere is it said that the most popular constitution (cash in the valuta position) should be abolished; it is only said that their advantages can also be attained by other means, and that they are clearly in decline. It seems that it was a necessary transit point, which we have to honor historically.

Consequently, the criticism should first have asked whether the monetary constitutions of England, Germany, France, and Austria can really be brought as special cases under the basic idea of nominalism. A counter-proof is not delivered, not even tried; It is admitted with some reluctance that a summary description of this point of view was, strangely enough, fairly well done. But that's the crucial point.

The criticism should have said: in fact, the payment system appears, viewed from the state, as it is described here.

And then the defenders of the bar constitution (the metallists in the sense of the journalistic, not in the theory) could have added: what luck, that the building is so spacious; Let us choose among the many possible forms of money the one which is the most expedient, the one that is most: we prefer the cash constitution of valuta money.

Did the critics do it that way? It does not seem that you have spoken of the dangers of nominalism, which exist, but which are not tempted by description; they want to reject the "theory of the state" as such, although it includes what the practitioners strongly recommend, and they almost felt it was a betrayal of the gold standard to describe and appreciate other currencies as well that we do not find the common justification of the gold standard very profound, but rather more solid reasons: in short, they have spoken as journalistic practitioners, and their last ulterior motive has always been that the "state theory" may have a tendency to shatter the well-tried good and very questionable trying to set in motion.

Beware of innovations and subtleties! A fairly simple cash-based financial system remains the best!

The whole dispute is so easy to solve: admit that theoretical metallurgism has not been enough to present the legal constitution of payment, and that recent developments are actually pushing cash into exodromic use and working towards artificially regulating the inter-valutary rates. But then explain that this should not be, and that we want to persist at an older stage. You can talk about that. Then it will soon turn out, Whether the exaggerated estimate of the bar constitution is strong enough to stop the development or not; it will not be strong enough, we say; it will be strong enough, you say. So here's the richest stuff to argue with.

But that one can challenge a description of what is by recommending what should be there - the representatives of the "state theory" will never admit that.

Postscript.

In the meantime, Wilhelm Lexis, without doubt the greatest expert in the field of monetary affairs, has made his judgment on the theory of the state (Archiv für Sozialwissenschaft, Vol. 23, Hert. 2, September 1906). As it is called page 572:
"The work represents the results of an intensive work of thought and will force its place in the scientific literature in its peculiar one-sidedness."

Page 574: *"But there are several new experiences that the metalist can hardly come to terms with. "*
Ibid. On the actual paper money: *"One can therefore no longer be content to anathematize it as a 'bad' money, but Knapp was entitled to start from a different concept of money, which includes the autogenous as the hylogenic money types."*

We give these sentences to the metallists and note that there are still theoreticians.

Among the practitioners, Dr. L. Calligaris in Vienna first

placed on the ground of the state theory; especially in the Austrian Rundschau, Volume 7, Issue 80, May 1906. September 27, 1906.

The currency issue from the state point of view
(On May 1, 1907, the author gave a speech as Rector of the University of Strasbourg and gave a lecture in the Statistical-Economic Society of Basel on May 4, 1907. The content of both lectures was written above in the work of the author "State Theory of Money", Leipzig 1905.)
[From Yearbook for Legislation, Administration and Völkswirtschaft, Volume X XXI (1907).]

Content.

It is not really about the material (gold, silver, paper), but about facilities for fixing the exchange rate against important neighboring countries. Today the gold standard serves this purpose, but within the country more money than is necessary is circulated; Nominal money would suffice for internal circulation, especially since central banks are beginning to regulate exchange rates.

The currency question!

Anyone who hears this quote immediately thinks of three things: gold, silver, paper. And the vast majority of newspaper readers will summarize their thoughts as follows: paper is bad, silver is better, gold is best.

Not so easy is the judgment of the experts, especially in the very latest time, since we have left the harmless individualism and have moved the position of the state in the development of payments in the foreground. As self-evident as the men of the eighteenth century, for example Adam Smith in 1776, think of it, unfortunately it is not, and today we are forced to penetrate a little deeper in order to fully understand the institutions of finance.

Is it possible to account for some kind of accountability?

Certainly only if we leave the difficult details aside and highlight only the most important.

First, what does an educated person think when asked about the nature of money? "The money," he says at once, "is a general commodity, and by far the most important case is that metals are recognized as such commodities, and in recent times chiefly the two precious metals, silver and gold." Here comes a fork: the one thinks of silver as the common commodity; other goods then have as value the amount of silver that is exchanged for a certain quantity of the good. The other thinks of gold as the common commodity; other goods then have as value the amount of gold that you receive in exchange for it.

But who has introduced the silver - or in the other case the gold - into the role of barter? "That's what the people did. the people, by doing bartering; even shorter: the traffic."

That this was done by a general vote is not exactly said, but one must almost surmise it: only then does the state come and obey the commandment created by traffic.

The value unit is then the weight unit of the metal, which is recognized as a general exchange good; for example, the pound of silver; or the pound of gold.

However, weighing is necessary; Everyone has a balance with them; You pay by weighing the metal to the receiver.

To cut this short, the state makes most useful: it creates coins, weighed and labeled pieces of that metal. These coins are money, while previously the raw metal was already a means of payment but not yet money.

This is the common view and insight into the monetary system. It is the view of the metallists, the monometallists. Beside them, the bimetallists have been around, since about 1869: both precious metals are equally worthy of being used as a commodity; according to their value ratio; a most simple thing, provided that gold and silver have their own lasting value.

If one gently points out to these three metalists that there is also paper money, unredeemable paper money, with which certain states operate for whole ages without sinking - then there is a pause of embarrassment; hesitantly they call the word credit. And now the metalist overflows with a wealth of positive knowledge, which, taken individually, may be all right, but which lacks any inner connection and closed structure; the listener is confused and impressed: I do not understand that; but the other one will understand it well, so let's leave it to the professional.

How does the state theory of money come about? Does she say yes or does she say no? Are the metalists right or wrong?

Answer: the melallists only examine a part of the phenomena presented by legal history. But one must look at the fullness of historical facts. The metallists are only right in so far as they envisage the beginnings of development. Therefore, every listener willingly inclines to those expositions. But that these explanations are too narrow, consider only the simplest cases and are wholly inadequate for the present condition of the monetary system, which the layman can not see through so quickly. Therefore, the natural man remains a metalist. He lacks an overview. Even more than that, it does not feel the need of everyone to reduce the whole abundance of phenomena to a single idea.

Most people are content with juxtaposing the thousands of facts piled on needles in their collection boxes with each other, as scholarship does, but science does not end this, but begins it. A truly general theory must not ask what this or that writer, this or that party, this or that school is advising, because the advice comes only last. On the contrary, one has to ask how states act in the field of money; which laws, ordinances and decrees they issue, and what common thought can be deduced therefrom.

When this is done - but not before - the moment comes, among the many possibilities to choose the best. Only then, at the very end, will the theorist become a counselor.

All money constitutions, which the layman divides according to the material of the plates (thus "gold currency, silver currency and paper currency"), go back to a basic idea, namely to this: the unit of value in each state is a legal, only historically defined term: the mark is the German unit of value, the franc in France, the ruble in Russia. These terms are everywhere defined by the connection with the former unit of value. Our mark, for example, is defined as a third of a Taller.

This historical definition is so broad that metal use is neither required nor excluded. It can not be otherwise if the common basic idea is to be developed, and indeed for all states, for those with gold currencies for those with silver currency and those with paper currency.

There is no generally applicable way to define the value unit by metal quantities.

This is certainly very strange philosophically; but this sentence is only to be mentioned fleetingly. On the other hand, we give a closer look to the practical side and highlight what is remarkable in monetary affairs in its recent development.

The following is generally known: England restored the gold standard after 1815, which was interrupted for a while at the time of the Napoleonic Wars. In the years 1871-1876, the German Empire adopted the gold standard. France had had bimetallism since 1803, but after the last war had become unfaithful to silver and, superficially, turned to the gold standard since 1876. In 1892 Austria began a long reform work whose initial aim has been evidently the production of the Gold currency. Thus, it is clear that silver currency is defeated as both bimetallism; the triumph of gold is undoubted; only on the metal gold the newer money constitution in the west of Europe is established. True, silver has not physically but legally lost its position as a precious metal; presumably because it is less suitable for money than gold. This is about what we have read countless times.

The fact of the triumph of gold is undeniable; but quite wrong is the widespread idea, as if in this case the properties of the two metals are involved, especially as if the lower usefulness of silver in the modern age have first been proven by practical experience. There can be no question of that. Nor is it true; that, for example, the popular opinion of those metals first changed, and that the governments then followed the changed popular opinion. These are all popular prejudices that are not valid.

To find the true reasons for the spread of the gold standard, we need to go further. What is actually gold currency? Is it the Constitution that makes larger payments in gold? It's not that easy.

Gold currency is rather a term that can only be defined if we determine in advance what cash money is and what valuta money is. Suppose that we are already clear about this, then the definition is this: only from the metal gold is money created; and this cash is put into valuta position: then you have gold currency.

But what is cash money?

All the people who are surprised by this question tend to answer: money made of precious metal is cash money; whether made of gold or silver, does not matter.
But our silver money, since the constitution of 1871, is no

longer cash; the Taler pieces are not, as little as the paper notes. To find the concept of cash, we do not have to start from physics but from legislation.

We ask: is there a metal that can be expressed in coins without restriction, in such a way that every pound of this metal is turned into pieces of definite validity?

With us since 1871 each pound of gold is infinitely convertible into pieces, which together amount to 1395 marks. For silver, this unlimited changeability is not covered; the Taler embossing is blocked; the coinage of the Reich silver coins is limited to certain amounts.

Therefore, there is only one kind of cash available: only our golden 20-mark pieces and 10-mark pieces are cash.
Of course we also have silver money; and silver is still, technically, a precious metal - but our silver money is not cash; it is - like the banknotes - nominal money; for there are also notional coins, which the layman does not know, although he easily recognizes the nominal nature of the copper and nickel coins.

Now we know what cash money is, and we have explained it in gold: If the silver were still unlimited, the bare silver money would also be explained. The metal is not so, but the laws of the transformation of metal into money.

Cash money is almost everywhere, even in countries with paper currency; In Austria, in addition to the unredeemable paper money, there was also cash money: formerly cash silver; since 1892 cash gold money. The mere existence of cash money is therefore not enough to come up with the concept of the gold currency or the silver currency. We still lack the idea of valuta money.

Every state has one kind of money, often several kinds of money, which are definite; that is, the payment in these types of money is final; there is no change, ex officio. With us the gold pieces are definite, but also the Talerstücke. Each payer has the choice of which of the definitive money he wants to use. The state as a payer also has this choice: whoever pays a salary must allow the state to accept the definite money that the state offers.

But which of the definitive types of money does the state actually use in its payments, in such a way that it keeps this kind always ready and, in the event of a dispute, not only offers it, but urges it?

The state occasionally offers us Talers, but he does not impose them on principle; keep ready and impose in case of dispute, he only does the gold money, we call such money valuta.

In Austria, the state keeps the banknotes ready and forces them on to the recipient of the payment: banknotes are therefore valuta.

To be valuta is therefore a quality that is recognized by the nature of state payment. Here it does not ask how the money is created, but how the state uses it as a payer.

Strange that this so important circumstance is recognized so late. And how incredibly important he is! For if the state declares that its payments, that is, the payments it makes as a debtor, are met with irreconcilable paper money, then he, the state, as court judge, must enforce that the paper is sufficient for private use. Otherwise the state as court judge would declare its own method of payment unfair!

So valuta is that kind of money, which keeps the state for its payments, in order to impose it in case of dispute.

Now it is easy to say which currency prevails in a country: search for the currency type; and then determine if she's barefaced or not.

In the German Reich, the gold coins are valuta money, and they have cash status, which, as we know, by no means applies to all types of coins. Our decision is therefore: we have gold currency.

Before 1871, the taler was valuta money, and at that time they had a bar constitution; now, of course, the talers have become urgent, but before 1871 they were cash: thus, before 1871, we had silver currency.

Since 1859, banknotes have been valued in Austria; It goes without saying that they are not-for-money, that is to say, not money. Thus, Austria, in layman's terms, still has the paper currency with important innovations, which are to be mentioned later.

These main features of currencies remain undisturbed by the many types of non-value-added, so-called accessory money. Our silver Taler does not disturb the gold standard, as long as the state can make its payments in gold when demanded. Likewise, before 1871, the then silver currency was not disturbed by the occasional "Friedrich d'or."

The maintenance of any cash currency presupposes that the state is in possession of the corresponding metal money; That is why, in times of distress, the cash currencies are sometimes trapped and replaced by notional currencies.

Now, if two states have in circulation a cash system of valuta money, then trade is easy.

But let us not forget one important condition: on both sides of the frontier, it must be barred on the basis of the same metal.

Between the Silver Land of India and the Golden Land of England, trade (before 1893) by no means went smoothly and surely, because it kept asking itself, how many rupees does the pound sterling cost today?

The trade profit still depended on it, after the purchase contracts were closed. The cheapest purchase could be highly lossy due to unfavorable movements in the exchange rate.

This brings us to the inter-valutary relations; and below is to be understood: the behavior of valuta money here to the valuta money there. This is not ordered by the states, but is originally an appearance of free circulation on the stock exchanges, thus a mercantile appearance. The supply and demand on the stock exchanges makes it clear every day how much Mark the Frank, the ruble, the pound sterling costs. This price, the so-called course, fluctuates back and forth, this is to be held above all as the self-evident; if the rashes up and down are small, there are special reasons for this.

So the interval currency rate varies by nature. For no state can enforce its own money for foreign territory.

The fluctuations of the exchange rate are usually very insignificant if both countries have the same cash structure for their valuta cash: for example, here as well as there gold currency; or here as there silver currency. The reason is easy to see: the money from here can be physically sent there and physically transformed into local money. After all, bar policy is based on the unlimited transformation of that metal into money.

Because of this strength of the exchange rate course, most writers want the gold standard to spread. A really practical formulation: of course much too narrow! At most, the theoretician may wish that bartering with the same metal would be widespread, that is, that either everywhere there would be gold currency or silver currency everywhere.

The reasoning of the bar constitution is this: if it rules on this side as well as beyond in the manner described, then the exchange rate courses fix themselves very easily. That is indeed their last reason. We are not afraid to say that the constitution of the Bar has no great significance for internal traffic. How else could it be understood that for decades, countries like Austria not only kept their valuta money in emergency form, but also prospered economically? But for the interstate relations, however, we must recognize the usefulness of the constitution of the Bar.
But how did silver get into the background since 1871?

Why exactly gold currency?

This has a significant historical reason. The dominant trading power in the year was England. England dominated the world market even then. England, however, had the gold standard and was reluctant to change its monetary system. Hence connection to England in the choice of currency metal. All other reasons are completely irrelevant and go past the main thing. Now we understand why we Germans left silver in the lurch. It was not silver; it was on the world market, and it belonged to the English.

If these reasons are correct, Austria must bring its golden cash into its valuta position as quickly as possible. But are the reasons right?

We always meet the same knot in the tangle of justification. The above reasons for the spread of the gold standard are not wrong, but they are only a special case of historical conditionality. The purpose is: fixing of the inter-valutary courses. This can happen among other things by consistent bar constitution. But there are perhaps other means that lead to the same goal - this has been recognized for some years and implemented in Austria and the Netherlands.

It is the state regulation of the inter-valutary courses by means of the stock exchange. Of this there is still little talk in our circles, as well known as the matter may be, and the great effect of the entire monetary constitution has been emphasized only recently with the necessary emphasis.

As we know, in 1892 the Austrian monarchy decided and

implemented a so-called gold loan, which brought in so much gold that it was possible to redeem all government notes - 312 million guilders - in the new crown money; or rather: could have redeemed. Of course, due to the interest, there is a need for an annual recurring burden on taxpayers; but the monarchy dared and succeeded. There was a tremendous amount of gold now; it became pronounced in pieces of 20 and 10 crowns. And now one would expect that the state notes would have been redeemed by the state and also the banknotes by the Austro-Hungarian bank, in the cash gold. Then gold currency would have been created, just as in 1858 a silver currency had been created for a short time.

But at the last moment they changed their minds: the paper statenotes were collected but replaced by other notional money, not gold coins at all; and the banknotes were not redeemed in gold coins.

And what did you do with the gold pieces? In part, they have been transferred to the bank to repay old debts; in part, the state keeps them imprisoned or makes them available to the bank for certain purposes, and these purposes are: regulation of the inter-valutary courses! Since the bank does not need to redeem its notes, this institution can use its own gold and other gold for that purpose. The bank is monitoring the rate, say between Vienna and Berlin, and as soon as the normal par value of 1 krone = 85 pfennig changes noticeably, the bank starts a counter-speculation to restore the pari.

Just as that airship on Lake Constance repeatedly restores the horizontal position of its longitudinal axis by a laurel weight, as soon as an undesirable deviation occurs.

However, gold is needed for these systematic counter-speculation, as is now the constitution of the Western countries, which have a gold standard; but you do not need to remove as much gold as you would need to make the bar constitution.

Nevertheless, the purpose is achieved: internally the bar constitution has no importance, and to the outside it is only useful because of the quiet inter-valutary courses. Now if these courses are brought to rest in another way - why should Austria change its present constitution of the monetary system?

The redemption of the local banknotes in cash, that is, in pieces of gold, is unnecessary, historically obsolete, and by no means corresponds to the real needs.

But what does this mean for the German Reich? Should we stop paying cash, as has happened in Austria since 1859? That was far away. Such changes occur through political constraints that have been spared us so far. There is no reason for us to take this step, and let us hope that in future wars we will not end up in such a predicament.

We can learn a great deal from the Austrian experience, for example, that the cash payments for internal traffic are by no means as important as one would expect in the memory of Baron von Bruck (1858). At that time everyone believed the need for bar traffic inside.

And today? The insight spreads that emergency traffic is sufficient in the interior, also here with us, while still maintaining the redeemability in cash. Pay attention only to the following signs: very recently, we have created banknotes of 50

Mk. And 20 Mk., Whereas in the past only 100 Mk. Were given. The justification heard everywhere is that the internal traffic should not take up so many gold pieces; that means: scriptural money is enough.

Furthermore, it is to be read in all specialist papers that it is a pity that the state draws so many pieces of gold from the Reichsbank every quarter of an hour for the payment of salaries; this would weaken the gold stock in the center.

Are not these noisy signs of how the verdict changes?

The former bar addiction is dwindling; the banking and stock exchange districts will soon become accustomed, and they will soon get used to justifying this by the fact that we can regulate the inter-valutary rates with us and have them regulated by the Reichsbank. Only then will the administration of the financial system be completed.

It also guarantees that one does not fall into adventurous attempts. After all, every serious man is rightly a little afraid of the emergency money (of course only in front of the paper), since it can be recklessly increased; therefore it threatens the inter-valutary course; our money could go down compared to foreign. It's like the fear of explosive substances; You just have to understand how to handle powder and gun cotton. That's why it does not occur to anyone to demand reckless increase of the emergency allowance without any addition: we only say: The emergency money will also be harmless to outside traffic if we add careful observation of the intervallular courses and determined counter-speculation to maintain the threatened parity. Of course, a completely impoverished state can not do that; but well-managed states can.

I am firmly convinced that we do not need as much gold in the German Reich as we spend now. It is as if one were accustomed at court to eat only of golden dishes; fine porcelain would do the same service; and the gold that has become redundant - not everything, but a large part of it - would be given freely for higher purposes.

Not gold and not silver are the essence of money; but these two metals are only the substances that were first turned into money by the state. Therefore, the state is also able to work the miracle of paper money, which remains completely incomprehensible as long as the state blind metalist feels it.

The question of currency is not the question of the use of gold and silver or paper in the monetary system, but is the question to which foreign states we wish to establish firmness of the interdepartmental course; the means for this purpose are less important; But the purpose itself today is this: we need fixed courses against England; and we will achieve this goal by using emergency money in internal traffic and by entrusting our Reichsbank with the regulation of inter-valutary rates.

About the theories of the monetary system.
Lecture, held in the Legal Society at Leipzig on December 30, 1908.
(From Yearbook for Legislation, Administration and Economics, Volume XXXIll (1909.)]

Content.

Two types of theoreticians: programmatic and analyzing. - The main thing is the administrative order of the monetary system with the political objectives of fixing the inter-valutary courses. - The international treaties actually want to be pari-profits. - Austria dropped the pari-plan of 1857; Italy has realized the ideas of the Latin Monetary Confederation.

In the field of economics there are many kinds of theories; We want to take a closer look at two of them: the programmatic theories and then the analyzing ones.

Every programmatic theory sets a goal to be realized, for example, the abolition of private landed property.

All oratorical means are mobilized to recommend this goal until it is implemented by the legislation. Another example is the introduction of the state-sponsored productive cooperative: the great orator Louis Blanc and his successor Ferdinand Lassalle have dedicated themselves to spreading this theory.

A very modern example would be the nationalization of mining operations. The programmatic theoreticians, as you can see, want to realize a practical goal.

It is well known that since 1870 two programmatic directions have been noticeable in the field of finance: the agitation of the bimetallists is still in the memory of contemporaries; more successful was the agitation of the gold currency men, whose most important leader was the deputy Bamberger.

Almost all teachers of economics have acted as programmatic theorists for the introduction of the gold standard. As the historical situation was after 1870, they were right; they have been charitable and can look back with satisfaction.

In order to effectively recommend this programmatic goal, they have all relied on the teachings of the so-called classical economics. With Adam Smith and David Ricardo they found a money theory that was quite metallic. There it is taught that the unit of value (sterling) is definable as a weight of metal; originally as a silver amount, later as a certain amount of gold.

This idea was easily accepted by our economists, and so they could most easily support their programmatic theory. Not only do they recommend the gold standard because it is useful; but they are also added because theoretical economics can not conceive of anything but a metallically defined unit of weight.

The involvement of programmatic theorists in such matters is significant, if only because the journalist and the deputy do not have time to delve into the study of pending matters. He wants to look up works that work for him; therefore, he uses the scholarly writings as an advice, and in this way the views of the school penetrate into public opinion. Once this has been achieved, the relationship is reversed: one relies on public opinion and finally claims that we have passed over to the gold standard, because this is grounded in the psychic life of the people; because the people demand a metallistically defined, now even a Gold-metallist defined unit of value. Whether that is true has no practical meaning. Since all programmatic theoreticians are based only on oratorical effect, they may at least choose the reasoning that "pulls." Strong reasons are the best, even the only practical ones, for the speaker.

I acknowledge, as I have said, without reservation that our economists have earned merit by their programmatic commitment to the gold standard, which was carried out by us in 1876. For since 1876 the Reichsbank has made its payments in our gold pieces as soon as the recipient insists on them; she does in fact, although until 1907 she would have been entitled to pay in Talers.

All that matters is that the Reichsbank pay in gold, at the request of the consignee. This has happened since 1876. Today she does too, and so we have long since achieved that goal.

But what is the use of this gold standard? In any case, that we now have firm courses against England, as well as against the other countries with gold currency. Fixed prices on the stock exchange; In other words: for one pound sterling one pays nearly 20.43 Mk on the stock exchange in Berlin.

Should the price be higher, we will send our gold pieces across the Channel, where they will be convertible into sovereigns on a fixed rate. If, on the other hand, the price is lower, the English send their Sovereigns to us, where they can be converted into 20-mark units according to fixed rates. Everyone admits that!

Our programmatic theorists claim even more; they say: now in Germany the unit of value, called Mark, can be defined by the assertion: a mark is the 1395th part of a pound of gold. Because from one pound of gold 1395 marks are struck in gold pieces, which no one doubts.

But this definition of the mark, that metallic definition based on the technique of currency, does not admit to everyone.
For example, I do not admit it, although it would be extremely effective to step on this metallic ground. It does not matter to me which reasons I support, if they only "pull". Because I'm not a publicist, not a programmatic theorist, but an analyzing. It is permissible to make this direction a little clearer, since it does not make sense in the first place.

The analyzing theorist stands in the auditorium and not on the political stage. He goes to the theater every day, so to speak, and looks at all the pieces; he says: everything we see there is worth studying. Other people have their favorite pieces and praise about only the magic flute or cabal and love; but they may not want to know anything about Richard Wagner. But our spectator says: a poet is not the same as all poets. Poetry as such must be studied in the totality of poets. Thus, the analyzing theorist is tuned in monetary matters.

There are a variety of monetary systems: gold currency, silver currency - even currencies with unredeemable paper. Some are worse, others better; but they all deserve to be described and explained first. **And above all, what all those system have in common? They must have something in common, much as the class of mammals has something in common.**

This common element completely misunderstood the otherwise quite respectable classical national economy, which in its time was not bad at all; on my account in excusable way; but completely misunderstood. She sees the common in coinage; from there it takes its exit, because in fact the coinage historically forms the beginning. All of our economists are metallists because they stop at the monetary start. They speak of fineness, of shot and grain, of character, of the sweetheart, of the passing weight - of absolutely necessary but also very technical things. As soon as the paper money, especially the unredeemable, appears, our economists are at a loss; they get into perhaps quite useful indignation - but they do not come. Coinage does not lead to the understanding of the financial system.

And why? Because the monetary system can only be understood by the payment system. But **the payment system is a legal matter**, while coinage is something technical.

Then the lawyers should be delighted to be asked to enter the hall from which the scholars of the coin are expelled. Certainly, if there were a lot of philosophically-minded lawyers. But as long as the lawyers only want to know what is legal in money matters today, they are indifferent. The judge simply asks: Can you make a valid payment in Talers? It used to be; now you can not do it anymore. And that's the deal. Next, only the philosophically-minded lawyer - of whom many consider the burden of reflection as necessary, but on the economists shift. That's the way it is now.

So you should go out of the payment system; Is not that a tautology? Is it possible to pay differently than with money?

Of course you can. When you paid even with groomed metal, you paid, but not with money.
Furthermore: if you pay by transferring a sight deposit, you pay, but not with money.

So there were payments before there was money; there would still be payments if there was no more money; but there are also payments with money.

So every general theory must speak; each of the three special cases would be far too narrow to serve as the basis of a theory. Equally cold-blooded, the analyzing theory goes on to further differentiate the money types.

Certain types of money are coins, so metal plates; marked with signs, so heavy; and certain other types of money are, technically, paper notes. "Hopefully redeemable", the melallist throws in. "Hopefully" - all right. But there is also unredeemable paper money; compare Austria since 1848, with only a very brief interruption. "But you can not make a real payment with that," says the metallist, saying that for 60 years now there has hardly been a correct payment in Austria!

And yet Austria has continued to live, who can not see that the metallists are falling into an impasse? If they only talk about coinage, they can not get beyond coinage, but we, who start with the legally imaginary payment system, we can still say: apparently, the payment system is another term than the metallists admit.

Now the programmatic theorist says: "Aha, one wants to worsen our monetary system", and all that is missing is that he calls the police.

Good heavens! Because you have programs, you think there is only programmatic thinking. One will be allowed to say how it was in Austria. This condition must be explained. The explanation is very simple.

It is not wonderful that one can pay with irreconcilable paper money, and that is because the payment does not necessarily depend on the transmission of a precious substance. This idea is just too narrow; it is autometallistic, that is to say, it is still believed to be in the original state of the tradition of balanced quantities of metal.

In Austria one pays with pieces which have the juridical property that the state asserts them as so many crowns when it has to receive payments. These pieces are of paper, of course. **But this paper has the property of being able to pay its taxes with it; this is certainly not a physical property, but it is a legal one.** The payment system in Austria is based on this. **There, then, numbers are an administrative phenomenon; it presupposes a state that gives laws and regulations** and that has a central bank. With this machine of mutual settlement one gets through there, and the technical machinery of expression is left, so to speak, only from the old times.

There can be no talk of a metallic definition of the Austrian guilder. It is based on the fact that there are debts in the traffic, which are measured in "gulden", and **gulden as a means of payment is any piece that is administratively recognized as a repayment of a debt**, regardless of whether this piece is a coin or a piece of paper.

Of course, the exchange rate against the neighboring countries, where you have cash payments, remains completely uncertain. Therefore, every cautious politician rejects this state. We too do it; only we have learned from this constitution that there is an administrative order of the payment system, while the school opinion speaks only of the coinage.

The analyzing theorist is now spurred on to think. Let us examine whether in the end we have the administrative mechanism. Let us take the German means of payment: the gold pieces, formerly also the Talers, then the silver coins, the nickel and copper coins, the rainbow banknotes and the banknotes.

A look at the laws and the regulations is enough to convince us: where payments to the state are to be made, all these pieces are accepted as so many marks: they are authoritative!

Payments to the state do not depend on intrinsic value; even not with gold pieces as long as they are still recognizable. It follows that we also have a similar apparatus of administrative law, just as in Austria. Of course, there are many more besides; For example, the redeemability of our notes, which is missing in Austria. With us, both cash and banknotes can be redeemed.
That justifies an important difference. Nevertheless, the similarity remains that the basic idea of administrative law in both states coincides.

Now let us concede that it is a theoretical need to systematically survey the monetary conditions of both countries.
Then the common must be put on top; and the facilities there, as well as the facilities here, must be regarded as special cases

of the common. Just as in zoology; if the animal forms are to be systematized, horse, bear, and lion appear among the mammals. And **if we now ask what is common to the Austrian constitution and ours, it turns out that the common feature lies in the salt of administrative law, which prescribes the state acceptance of the pieces.**
The state creates such administrative law. Therefore, we call the theory of monetary system, which systematizes all phenomena of payment, with complete rest, "the state theory of money."

Its content is not the recommendation of the imperfect state which Austria once offered; but only systematic accommodation of the same. Even the most decided enemy of paper money must allow the description of this device - and more is not required. Rejecting the systematization is quite impossible; it would be as if the lions, bears, or horses refused to be counted among the mammals.

At the same time, the economist is still allowed to reject certain monetary constitutions; He may have very sufficient reasons for this; in particular, he may continue to condemn the paper money economy; but to exclude them from the system would really only be childish anger or intellectual helplessness. For history has produced this constitution in countless cases.

Anyone who simply rejects the state theory of money, he certainly lusts it for a very practical reason, thus acts as a programmatic theorist: he is more comfortable in combating the dangerous constitutions of payment by excluding them from the system. If he admits them in the system, then he must justify his fight in ways other than the usual way, and for this purpose he must rearrange his thoughts differently. Some metallists have admitted this quite calmly, but only conversationally, which deserves all recognition, as any act of sincerity.

The assertion that there can only be a metallic monetary system is therefore only a veiled desire, of the content: "Would only there be metallic constitutions!"

But on the other hand, the practically effective person is quite right when he says: well, you only systematized for the time being; but what do you recommend, you representatives of the state theory of money? That's the main thing for us.

We recommend exactly what the metallists want in the deepest sense; but we recommend it for other reasons, and we formulate the goals in a different, more general way. Let's listen to what the metallists have demanded, depending on the situation, and try to improve the formulation.

From 1857 to 1859, the Austrians rightly restored the silver currency; however, she soon fell into disrepair again; but let's listen to those two years once. It was the time of the reforms of Baron von Bruck. Metallistically the reasoning reads as follows: the Austrian unit of value must become definable as a certain quantity of silver; so we are proposing new silver gulden pieces at 45 for one pound sterling, and the state will pay for it on request.

So redemption of banknotes. Then the exchange rate on German places will be such that the gulden on the stock exchange is always to be 2/3 Taler. The success really came in 1858. So the silver metalists were practically right.

However, state theory says: the most important thing of the reform is that the gulden of Austrian currency always has the price of 2/3 Talers on the stock exchanges. You have achieved this in your own way by the means of cash payment. That was an effective, so a good remedy; but any other means would have been admissible if the same result had been achieved.

Maybe there are such other means; and if not, your reasoning was wrong; because the metallistic definition of the guilder is wrong because it completely failed for the period before 1857. You have set that definition only to recommend the cash payment. It was practically effective, but your theory was too narrow.

In 1892 a new order of money was necessary in Austria. Then the metallists said: Let's go over to the gold currency. Let's create gold pieces, from the pound fine 3,280 kroner, that's half gulden. With these pieces of gold should then be paid. The banknotes are to be redeemable on demand in the golden crown money. The unit of value crown is thus now to be defined metallistically as a certain amount by weight of gold.

But sooner the silver should be used; why then suddenly gold? Answer of the Metallists: The silver has become useless. Only the gold has the required properties internally. The silver had now come to be affected by rickets, as sometimes healthy children lose their straight limbs. Now we metalists believe only in the gold.

They also say: Then we will have fixed exchange rates against Germany; it was from now on that the gulden on the stock markets was set at 1.70 Mk.

On the other hand, state theory says: You want to set up a monetary system in Austria in such a way that the Austrian guilder is always available on the stock exchanges for 1.70 marks.

This decision is praiseworthy, inasmuch as all fluctuations cease, for this purpose you have created your golden crown money. If the state always pays, then you reach your goal. Nevertheless, with the new metallic definition of the crown it is nothing, for similar reasons as there was nothing in 1857 with the silver-metallic definition of the guilder. Meanwhile, let's see if you have gone to cash or not.

And what happened? Austria has not yet transferred to cash in gold. The golden pieces of 10 and 20 crowns are locked up; Nobody has the right to cash banknotes in gold.
That's true, says the metalist; but the reform is not finished yet, the main thing is coming!

But the state theory answers: You will probably wait in vain; for the main thing is indeed accomplished; Without cash, the Austrian price on the stock exchange is fixed, it is 1.70 Mk for the guilder! Why then cash payment?

What a surprise! The metallists knew only one means for the laudable goal; But the praiseworthy goal was attained by practice in another way, and now the metalist is angry.

One thinks here of the young Roland, who slew the giant while his far wiser father slept.

The impartial practitioners in the Vienna Ministry of Finance and in the Austro-Hungarian Bank have reached the attachment of the German-Austrian course, until now without cash payment in gold. This seems much more deserving to me than the one-sidedness of the metallists who, as programmatic theorists, glorify a school opinion that is far too narrow and actually only has the advantage of being easy to understand because it meets the prejudices of the crowd.

Among these prejudices is the low regard for the participation of the state in all questions of economic development. All you have to do is pronounce the word "state", and you will already come across an instinctive dislike of all the representatives of the classical trend, who always only want to hear something from the people.

In particular, the institutions of the monetary system should, according to them, emerge from the people as such! One even hears say, "the people make their means of payment." Does this really do the people without the participation of the state?

Or does the state follow the people only as a subordinate position, as it were, merely as an editor of the ideas that have been permeated by the people?

One should almost believe that this is the opinion of the metallists. My opinion is not. **In the theory of money, one has to step on the new ground, which is the study of the really given administrative law of the important states.**

Very uncomfortable indeed!

How much more comfortable is the timeless and place-less essence of the popular philosophy that our listeners love so much! But who takes it seriously? Only those who know or can not know otherwise.

Perhaps one gradually admits that the state theory offers a tolerable systematization of the monetary constitutions; but this is only a formal privilege, a legally tempting treatment, but let the whole economic treatment aside. The economist wants factual truths; he can not do anything with formalism, he says.

This is true, however, that **economics is not confined to the theory of money; Apart from the nature of money, it is also necessary to talk about how the money economy works. One wants to be informed about the nature of banking, one wants to know what exchange traffic means, or why one or another of these discount policies is driven.** Of course, that should happen; but this does not justify remaining in the nature of money on a popular-philosophical basis, **as if the economist were allowed to work here with completely inadequate means.** The theory of money is not imaginable without what is called formalism.

But above all, consider this: however formalistic the State Theory of Money may be, it is not merely formalistic, but contains the basic political thought which is increasingly emerging as the actual content of monetary policy. What is this basic idea?

More recently, all states want the same thing; they want to

fortify the interdepartmental course against the economically important neighboring countries. So, for example, Germany should set the highest possible rate for the French franc, for the British pound sterling. This is not only convenient for the trade, it is also advisable because of the accommodation of government bonds, Just think about how much Austria is interested in the accommodation of its public debt in the German Reich!

So the course fixation is the main idea of our monetary policy. But there are many resources. In the past, one knew only one thing: one introduced state cash payment everywhere and chose the metal that underlies the cash in England; then the courses against England settle easily, almost by themselves. The advice was good; it was followed by us in 1876; and also the other states developed their monetary system in this direction. Hence the victory of the gold standard.

Why does Austria not follow this rate? That's because a different regulation of courses against England has been invented by practitioners. There, the bank has decided to act as a "strong hand" on the stock exchange and to destroy every incurring deviation from the pari by deliberate counter-speculation.

So it regulates the price of English means of payment - not only the exchange of letters, but at all the English means of payment - and this activity has been successful. If this is not possible in the long run, then perhaps one comes back to the plan of cash payment; I do not believe it; because now it would have no purpose, since the goal - namely attachment of the course - has already been reached.

The State Theory now enters this attempt without prejudice and thus becomes highly independent of earlier well-intentioned advice; it just asks for the target, so it is not against the gold standard; but only as long as the gold standard, as this constitution serves that purpose, as it is the case with us. If the gold is no longer necessary for this purpose, the State Theory leaves this metal as cold-blooded out of play as it now lets the silver out of play. We are not here to give money to one or another metal; but in order to organize our monetary constitution appropriately and vote respectively for the purpose metal - or for any other means of course attachment.

As a defender of this theory in the press are most zealous: L. Calligaris in Vienna and dr. Friedrich Bendixen in Hamburg, both known as men of banking. Numerous younger forces have already joined them.

[Dr. Ludwig Calligaris, Government Councilor, official of the Austro-Hungarian Bank in Vienna, is the author of the work: The new currency and bank accounts (Die neuen Valuta- und Bankgesette). Vienna 1901 (Manz law edition, 16th volume). His article in the Supplement to the Allgemeine Zeitung, Munich, February 1, 1906, The State Theory of Money, is the earliest understanding discussion of the work I have published under the same title (Leipzig, 1905) Of the numerous other articles The same author is still mentioned in the Austrian Rundschau, vol. V 11, vol. SO, May 10, 1906, which bears the same title.
Calligaris has contributed above all else to the fact that the State Theory of Money has attracted attention in Austria.

Dr. jur. Friedrich Bendixen Director of the mortgage bank in

Hamburg, has published: The essence of money (Das Wesen des Geldes). At the same time a contribution to the reform of the Reichsbank legislation. Leipzig 1908, Duncker & Humblot. 60 pages. In this paper, the State Theory of Money is also welcomed with understanding. This is followed by further considerations, which are very remarkable but can not be discussed here.]

"So then is any course fixation right for you? After all, we metalists think, it depends on how high the fortification takes place. The Austrians have kept their guilder at the rate of 1.70 Mk. should not they have chosen the height of 2 Mk? Do not the Austrians lag behind the Italians, who have lately fixed their lira so that it equals the French franc on the stock market, while the lira has been much lower for many years? "

I am pleased to address this question, which has so far been under-discussed. The state theory will not leave us in the lurch. It depends here on the actual meaning, on the political meaning of the contracts, which are closed under the name of the German-Austrian Coin Contract and the so-called Latin Coin League. These contracts betray in their name the basic metallurgical concept, by not the money, but of coins is mentioned. This corresponds entirely to the then state of theory, but not today.

The legal interpretation of those contracts is quite simple. Italy adopted the then French system dating back to 1803. Legally, the contract has always been fulfilled; the Italians stamped the 5-lira piece out of silver, the 20-lira piece out of gold.

In France as well as in Italy you took the domestic money, but also the neighborly money in payment. This remained legal, even as Italy fell into the poorest paper currency and no one in Italy used those two types of cash. Still, one could then have paid in Italy both with silver 5-Lira or 5-frank piece, as well with 20-Lira or 20-Frank-piece; only one did not do it, since the state paid in paper money without redemption.

That's why the private people also paid in paper, and the course between Italy and France fluctuated back and forth. In spite of all the legal fulfillment of that treaty, the purpose of the Latin Coin League had been completely missed; because the contract had only called the insignificant, concealed the essentials.

The essential would have been this: France and Italy want strength of the course, so that Lira on the stock exchange has the rate of 1 franc. For this purpose, the Münzbund is closed. This is the political interpretation. Has this purpose been achieved? Not for a long time, because Italy was too weak. But for some years now, Italy, without cash, has raised the price of its lira by means of public funds so as to achieve that purpose.

This highly remarkable success means that Italy has always remained faithful to the Federal Treaty; but politically, fulfillment did not succeed until it fixed its course in the sense of that treaty.

Italy, therefore, has reached a course fortification which really corresponds to the intention of that treaty, but in which, out of theoretical clumsiness, the goal was not mentioned, but only subordinate means were enumerated. The Italian course regulation is therefore more than a mere attachment to the current state; it is a fortification according to the political meaning of that treaty; I acknowledge that Italy has achieved more than Austria.

In the German-Austrian Coin Contract of 1857 it is stated that Austria creates the new guilder, which has the silver content of 2/3 Talers.

This contract, in its very inadequate wording, has also been legally fulfilled. But what was the political purpose?

Obviously: on the stock market, the Austrian guilder should now have the rate of 2/3 Talers. This purpose has not been achieved at all since 1859 because of the insolubility of Austrian notes. The state paid in unredeemable paper; and the other people are doing it too. The guilder sank on the stock market well below 2/3 Taler.

Then, however, Austria recovered, and in 1892 began the reorganization of its finances. The market price of the guilder was fixed - but according to the actual state of the time, that is to 1.70 Mk., Not to 2 Mk. That simply means for us:
In 1892 Austria broke away from the political meaning of that coin treaty of 1857, after the question had already come to an end in 1867. It did not want to bring the sacrifices that would have been needed to restore the Pari of 1 guilder equal to 2 Mk. This is one of the consequences of the completely changed position of Austria to Germany since 1866. Therefore, in 1892, Austria was content with a fixation of the actual course, according to which the gulden should remain equal to 1.70 Mk and remained, waiving the goal of Bruck's reform.

With regard to Austria and Italy, the following difference now arises:
All the creditors of Italy, as far as they live in France, have been in the same situation for some years now, when the Latin Coin Confederation was shut down: what they receive from liras can be converted into as many francs.

The totality of the creditors of Austria, as far as they live in the German Reich, however, have not been restored to the position which existed in 1858. What they refer to gulden interest can not be translated into twice as many marks, but only in 1.70 times as many marks. These creditors, considered as a whole, have been distressed about it; they felt damaged. From which view of the legal situation? Obviously from this: they suggest that the reform of the Erh. von Bruck was not merely a coinage contract, but a so to speak eternal pari-contract. However, Austria rejects this idea, while it really did hold the coin contract as long as it existed.

Perhaps, due to improved insight, clearer contracts will be signed in the future. In any case, the time should be over when you closed such uncertainly tapping coin contracts.

However, the following consideration is more important for weeping:
Anyone who praises the procedure of the Italians and complains that of the Austrians can do so without using the completely inadequate justification of the Metallists. For the metallists do not have a sufficient idea of the so-called exchange rate, or rather of the inlervalutarian course.

The State Theory of Money, which really gives an account of the course of the Intervalutary courses and understands the adjustability of these courses, gives much better information about why Italy and Austria acted so differently.

Italy took the Latin Coin Confederation as a pari-contract and sought subsequently to satisfy its demands again; that was pari-loyalty!

Austria took the German-Austrian Coin Contract only as a coin contract and refused to recognize it as a pari-contract after it had been supplanted from the German State; it announced the pari-fidelity!

I will only say this about the usefulness of the State Theory of Money for the clarification of currency history: it has already been applied to England, France, Germany, and Austria, and more recently to Switzerland [Kurt Blaum, The monetary system of Switzerland since 1798. Strasbourg 1908, with Karl J. Trübner. 176 pages (treatises from the Political Science Seminar on Strasbourg, Issue XXIV); further Johannes Scheffler, The monetary system of the United States of America in the 19th century from the point of view of the state. Strasbourg with Karl J. Trübner. 123 pages (treatises from the Political Science Seminar on Strasbourg, Issue XXV). A similar work on Italy is known to me in the manuscript and will soon be published by Trübner; the author is Emil Franz, the title reads: The constitution of the state means of payment of Italy since 1861.], to the United States, to Italy nowhere fails; while the metallists have come to no sufficient representation of any country; they can not even explain the phenomena that are summarized under the term "agio," yes, they do not even have sufficient terminology and find it whimsical to create one, and despite their practical merits, they are lagging behind as theoreticians.

But why do they remain in their narrow thought-building?

That's because they are programmatic and non-analyzing theorists. This will take as long as they reject the legal view. A satisfactory theory of monetary affairs is only possible if juridical thinking is introduced in this field: for this purpose the state theory should give guidance.

Finally, I would like to draw attention to the most significant changes in the legislation, as far as the German Reich comes into consideration:
The Taler are no longer legal tender since October 1908; As you know, they are turned into Reichsilbermünze, to which the new Dreimarkstück is added.
Our banknotes, formerly restricted to pieces of at least 100 marks, are now also made in smaller pieces.
There is also general conviction that banknotes will soon be closed to legal acceptance of payments to public coffers, and perhaps to private transport, which, as we know, is still lacking.

All this indicates and point out that the development of the monetary system is still in flux with us; the goal to which we are heading is evidently: the spread of emergency money in internal traffic; Retention of solvency, as far as possible according to the political situation; but at the same time preparing the exchange-rate regulation of the exchange-rate course against the important states of foreign countries, as has already been done in Austria and Italy.

Austria and the state theory of money.
172nd Plenary Assembly of the Society of Austrian Economists, held on March 24, 1908.

From the "Volkswirtliche Wochenschrift" by Alexander Dorn.

On Tuesday, March 24, 1908, the Society of Austrian Economists held its 172st Plenary Assembly. On the agenda was a lecture by Dr. Ing. G. F. Knapp, Professor at the University of Strasbourg, on "Austria and the State Theory of Money." The President, Mr. Hofrat Prof. Dr. Philippovich, presided over the meeting with the following words:

We like to enjoy the great advantage, Prof. Dr. G. F. Knapp welcome from Strasbourg as a presenter. Professor Knapp is no stranger to us Viennese. There are numerous friends, disciples and supporters of Professor Knapp here in Vienna, and we therefore find it a special personal satisfaction that he did not shun the journey for us to appear in our midst and speak here. I believe that he too has a certain interest in Austria. He admonished us younger people - if I may still count myself among the younger ones - over and over again that we should remember ourselves as Austrians and observe and study the events here in the country. Now he has recently shown that in a field which is richest in history for the theory of economic theory new information can be obtained from the events in Austria. We are pleased that Prof. Knapp has just chosen this area to inform us about Austria's relations to the state theory of money today. We thank him for coming and warmly welcome him. I ask Prof. Knapp to speak up.

Welcomed with lively applause, Prof. Dr. Ing. G. F. Knapp take the word for the following explanations in free speech. (Stenographic report by Dr. Richard Kann. Compare the work: G. F. Knapp, State Theory of Money, Leipzig 1905.)

My revered present! Above all, I am tormented by the feeling that I am in an astonishing minority regarding my views. So I need some protection. I understand my situation here so that I am allowed to listen to my peculiarities. On the other hand, I renounce from the outset to convince someone. I would only like to suggest how I come to my opinion, which differs somewhat from the general accepted theory about the monetary system and from which corner these deviations seem necessary to me. But I'm far from expecting any approval.

At first I thought that it would be useful to talk about the question of accepting or refusing cash payments. Now my friend Philippovich and Mr. Ostersetzer have informed me that much has already been said and discussed in Vienna and especially in your society, and that this question is no longer considered very urgent. That's enough for me. I have therefore postponed this topic and want to deal more with the very general question of how to come to the so-called state theory of money, in my opinion.

If we take a close look at our textbooks, there is no doubt that the theories of the monetary system which are put forward essentially take their starting point from the point of view of coin history and coinage. The sentence that the gold must be mixed into so many and so heavy pieces that have a state stamp, or that the other metal, silver, so must be balanced, also with a state stamp, and then paid with these pieces It returns everywhere, so to speak, as the simplest and most natural thing, and from this sentence one goes up the ladder in rungs to finally explain the whole monetary system from the initial point of view.

Again and again it turns out that our coins are characterized as pieces whose weight and fineness are guaranteed by the state.

For some coins, however, this is true, but characterizes only the trade coin, such as the ducats, the Maria-Therese Taler: trade coins, with which you can not pay a cup of coffee in Austria, because they are not money. These coins are state-of-the-art pieces whose stamp really only means that and nothing else; Money is not these pieces; because they lack the legally stipulated validity in units of value. No one can tell from a ducat how many crowns he holds; it is not at all, it is a piece of gold, but not money.

What characterizes metal money as money is not the metal content, but the validity attributed to metal money by the state. Those writers who begin with weight and fineness and see in the stamp only an attestation of these technical qualities, I call metallists, This is not a rude expression (cheerfulness), but is to characterize that as the characteristic of the metal content of the pieces is meant.

On the other hand, I have invented the name of the Chartalists for those writers whose number is unusually low, and who do not assume the value, but rather the state affiliation, from the legal premise that this piece is considered by the state to be one or five or ten crowns It is meant that such government-sponsorship can and must not only take place in the case of coins, so that they circulate as money, but that this settlement can also be transferred to paper-slips. This is the beginning of the state theory of money, starting from the legal rule that determines the validity of the pieces. While the

prevailing theory of finance has a technical basis, this state theory has a legal, an administrative legal basis.
Now one might ask, why does one not remain with the first kind of the consideration, with the content of the pieces at gold, silver etc?

To which I reply that metallistic intuition can explain the beginnings of finance because they have really been so. No doubt: for the beginning of the monetary system, the metallic view is quite excellent, because it simply describes how one came to such means of exchange. But we are not quite in the beginning, but we are at least in the middle of the development of the financial system. It is important to the theorist to formulate his general propositions in such a way that one can derive not only a part of the development but the whole development from it. And there is no question for me that although the beginnings of finance are brilliantly explained from the metallic viewpoint, one can not find the middle and the end of development with them.

The history of the Austrian monetary system can be explained quite satisfactorily in some, albeit very short, epochs, for example, the history of the Austrian monetary system in the months of September to December 1858, when it was described to Baron v. Bruck was able to produce cash in Austria in the sense of the silver currency. For a few months Austria has had a monetary constitution that can also be understood, but not exclusively, metallistically. On the other hand, in the remaining, rather many years, both before and after the periods of the Italian war, there is an epoch for Austria, the phenomena of which are completely impossible to explain with metallic theory. It is useful only for the beginning, but not for further development, so it is not comprehensive enough to absorb the overall development, and for me that is proof that metallistic theory does not deserve the recognition it deserves takes up.

A theory that is too narrow is not a complete theory; for a complete theory must be far enough to accommodate all phenomena. But this is not possible with metallic theory if it is to be applied to Austria. After all, Austria is an empire whose manifestations also want to be explained, and because this is not possible with metallistic theory, I have broken with it.

One might think, for example, that I am an enthusiastic supporter of the very miserable paper money, and that so bad and quite a lot of paper money would be my ideal. Because that would be the idea realized that the money, these rags, have no value. But nothing is further from me than that. The thing is not that the state theory of money rejects metal money and only recommends paper money to make people happy. This is the pure understanding.

The non-metallistic theory, the Chartaltheorie, is not opposed to the metallistic theory, but superior. It is the wider term. The common house should be built in order to accommodate the different forms evenly. Anyone who thinks that I am a supporter of the exaggerated issue of paper money, of inflation and of such abuses, is completely mistaken. I take for granted that states can keep their budgets in order, I do not need to emphasize that.

I am by no means a friend of the Assignat economy. But for me there is a need to explain the Austrian phenomena; I do not want to recommend it any further, I just want to say how it happens that you can do that as well. That's simply because the legal moments are the main thing. The administrative equipment is much more important than the coin technical equipment, which is completely missing the paper money.

However, administrative law governs both metal money and paper money and offers something that is shared by both. In this respect, everything depends on the administrative law, and from this corner it will become clear why one can do business in Austria. If one managed unhappily here and there, it was wars or other unfortunate circumstances that led to financial embarrassment. These conditions have created the financial embarrassment, but not the paper money has done it, as the audience always means.

If one tries to understand the conditions as they have been in Austria, one will find that the terminology, which is based on metallurgical theory, is not sufficient for Austria. It is now a matter of finding new names for the administrative properties of money. In addition, a large part of my readers are greatly shocked. But if administrative law is to be used, administrative names must be introduced! What do we understand by cash, for example? Every layman says cash is money made of precious metal, gold or silver - nickel money is no longer cash. That's a technical definition. Cash is now administratively defined by the state theory of money, in such a way that the condition for cash is that a metal can be indefinitely defined. If the condition exists where the laws say that every quantum of gold or silver is de jure *pronounced in so many crowns or gulden, that is a legal proposition. This starts the consideration of what cash is.*

Then there is a coin-foot that says in how many units of value the pound of metal must be pronounced; for example, 45 guilders from the pound of silver. Cash is now that piece of money whose fineness corresponds to the base of the coin for free expression. These are definitions in terms of the law of litigation, in contrast to the technical definitions that speak for the master of the mint, but which do not explain the system of payment. The master of the mint is only a technician, like the engraver or the lithographer who makes our banknotes technically. The monetary system, of course, must have its background in its application for payment, otherwise it is not economically available.

As opposed to cash, the state theory uses the term "emergency money." Our nickel coins, although not made of paper, are distressed, our gold coins are cash, they are freely definable, today's silver coins are not cash, for they are no longer freely definable.

This is the administrative labeling, this must be strictly done and must not be mixed with the technical definitions, otherwise you can not understand the thing, It is impossible that the administrative law should not be here. But the administrative law involved in the question of money is badly neglected, because we only ever hear of the metallists swarming, be it gold or silver, or the bimetallists for both, while the legal side is less precise about the writers is taken. But the matter is not completely new. I have come to know a treatise by Friedrich Gentz dating from 1816, which elegantly casts into the audience a whole series of moments which state theory asserts. There are also newer writers in whom similar aspirations emerge, and it's all about doing it consistently,

For example, I would like to make it possible to cite another important distinction in monetary matters, which makes administrative law very tangible. Let's ask, what is valuta cash? The metalist will reflect on the question of the type of metal and on the monetary standard. Value money is but a purely legal term; it is that money in which the state as such, when it has to pay, makes its payments and, indeed, makes them intrusive. For example, in the last half of 1858, our well-known silver gulden, still in circulation today, was valuta money. Either the state paid in silver gulden at that time, then the thing was good, or he paid in banknotes, which were then redeemable. The definitive payment could therefore always be obtained in silver gulches at the request of the recipient. The silver gulden was valuta at that time. And what is valuta money today? Do not be frightened, gentlemen-it's the banknote. Our local banknotes are valuta cash. There is no legal rule according to which the state has submitted to the requirement that it pay that money.

If, for example, the recipient of the note says that I want to redeem them, the Austro-Hungarian Bank says: If we are comfortable, we will do it, but if you want to force us to do so, then we come to the paragraph in which it is said that a redemption does not take place. So we have as valuta money in Austria in the administrative sense, the banknote. It always depends on the position taken by the state in the various types of money available in one country. If tomorrow the Austrian government insists that the banknotes be redeemed in gold, the gold coins would be valuta money.

The property of valuta money is not attached to the material, but to what the layman can not see; the layman simply looks at the play; Of course, the taxi driver can not see the legal qualities.

What the audience means is completely indifferent; It is nonsense to give the least to the opinion of the public in the monetary constitution. It only depends on what the connoisseurs say.

Valuta money, since it is a matter of invisible legal relations, can not be externally recognized at all, but only in the position which the state takes in relation to the payments it makes. I go even further and raise the much more heretical view by saying: also the laws are not decisive, it depends only on how the state *acts. Just read the text of the 100-crown notes that are in your pockets (serenity). On these notes it says: The Austro-Hungarian Bank pays immediately upon request 100 crowns in legal metal money to the bearer with pleasure. Is he doing that? No. It does not matter what the note says; it only depends on what happens.*

As soon as the state executes the redemption, the gold money becomes valuta.

As soon as he does not make that redemption - whatever the banknotes and laws are - the gold is not valuta money. In 1859, without a special law being issued, the state simply paid notes, and subsequently said that these notes were also forced into the public eye. The action of the state is the deciding thing, everything else is the same. This looks heretical because the lawyers are accustomed to judge everything only from the laws.

But here the action decides.
Unlike valuta money, we call the other types accessory. Our gold coins are accessory, although they are made of gold.

It is a very common opinion, widespread everywhere and even among professors, that metal money has the property of maintaining a constant value. If you look in the notes, that's true. You can see this for many countries for decades. You can see this in England or Germany since 1876. The price list shows how much the kilo of fine gold costs, and we see that, practically speaking, this kilo of fine gold has an almost immutable value. Therefore, so the layman says, one must pass to the gold standard. Here, however, every syllable is the most complete error. Our gold has a very solid market price in Germany and other countries where the gold standard is fully implemented, as in England. But why? Because the invisible and unnamed administrative activity of the state is there, which gives the gold this firmness of the price. If, in Germany, one pound of gold produces 1395 Marks unrestrictedly, no one who has gold to sell will give away his gold at a cheaper price. In Germany and England banknotes are also redeemable in gold. I will therefore; if I act as a buyer of gold, I will pay no higher price for the same than results from the redemption of the notes. However, where there are two such facilities, namely an unlimited buyer at fixed prices and an unlimited supplier at fixed prices, then a fixed value arises.

In this way you can fix the prices for the petroleum, if you use such an organized price management. However, this has no name and is therefore often overlooked by the people. As a result, there are many people who do not quite turn conscious.

In the same way you can make the strength of the silver price if you want to make what you do in Germany with the metal gold with the metal silver. In 1858 silver had such a fixed price in Austria. How can one, as long as our theory of money still harbors the idea that gold has the property of keeping a fixed price, say that this is a trained theory? Here you can not see what is in the hidden paragraphs and taken together is a state institution, which had the strength of the gold price or earlier silver price result. And especially in the purely administrative perspective, this relationship must be clear, it can not remain hidden, it can only be hidden if you only consider the coinage.

The not very young gentlemen among us still remember the silver agio *before 1878 and later the gold agio of the years 1892, 1893 and 1894. Now nobody talks about it anymore. Today, only the scholars know what this so-called agio means - for the sake of simplicity I only want to speak of the silver* agio. *This agio is extremely easy to explain from the administrative point of view. But it can not be explained from the standpoint of the metallists. The valuta money types have no* agio. *They are always delivered by the state. On the other hand, the accessory types of money which run alongside the valuta money sometimes lose their premium. The silver gulden had in 1860 an agio of about 20%; The silver gulden was then, in 1860, not value-for-money, but accessory money. It was paid in paper, which was not redeemable.*

The silver gulden always counted for a gulden, just as the gulden today is considered a gulden, because this validity was granted to the gulden by state law. Now, all that is needed is a boom, according to which the width of the plate is greater than the state of the piece. In this way, the complicated question of the Agio *can be solved with ease. For the validity of the pieces does not depend on the value of the plate, the validity of the pieces is something juristic, but the value of the plate is a phenomenon of the metal market. This was especially evident in 1878, when the former agony of the silver gulp suddenly disappeared and turned into a* Disagio *that the owner of the plate would have suffered if he had used the gulden as a plate, as a piece of silver for silvering, and so on , - If it is permissible to draw a perimeter within which a theory applies and that which falls outside of this circle is stamped as an exception to this theory, then one can give up immediately the business of the theoretician. Rather, a theory must be so arranged that even the most difficult phenomena can be explained by it; otherwise it is not a theory.*

A theory must be such that even so-called abnormal, hitherto incomprehensible phenomena can be explained. I must demand a theory that it be generalized until such inconceivable phenomena can be put in the right place and inserted into theory. Everything else is just theory - if I may say so - in the sense of a layman. It is the stubborn ride on too narrow a train of thought, is perhaps a feat but not a theory. Another achievement of state theory is the following:

I know of no other theory that gives a real account of the nature of exchange rates. There is much talked about and written about the exchange rates, but it is usually started metallically and the result is therefore not completely completed. Anyone who writes about it usually thinks of two countries with as simple a constitution as possible; For example, in one country he gives the gold currency and the other the silver currency. Then the exchange rate, the ratio of the unit value in one country to the value unit in the other country, is explained as the value ratio of silver and gold. This is such a mystical cloud that sends us its lightning, and our economic life - one must always choose very high-sounding expressions (cheerfulness) fatalistically controlled. Such a fatalistic value ratio, which would direct our exchange rates, does not exist. It is not only possible to study exchange rates for the specific case of countries with gold and silver currency, but to leave the different countries open to the most diverse forms of money.

As is well known, Austrian money is worthless in Germany, and German money is not considered a bright place in Austria either. Our money, taken in the legal sense, does not apply at all abroad; it can, legally speaking, not be used as a means of payment there. The term validity is tied to the state. Outside the state concerned, the coin is no longer money. And only the exchange rate teaches us how the money of one state is exchanged for money of the other state. But that is a matter of stock exchange traffic. There are no mysterious relationships of gold and silver floating in the air, but the stock market determines how much lighter the mark is and how much pfennig the crown. From this results then the value relationship of the precious metals, as long as such precious metals are convertible into money, thus in certain states at certain prices their buyers have.

I know of no description of exchange rates that would not be vitiated by the error, that only a few special cases are discussed, albeit quite brightly, without the principle underlying the whole being worked out. This is only possible if one always remembers that the administration of a coin is a juridical property bound to the state in question, that the same thing is again the case in the other state, and that only between these two states there is a bridge: stock market trading, supply and demand. People always want to pretend that there is a fixed exchange rate per se. But that does not exist. The exchange rate is by nature a wavering thing that can only be fixed by special circumstances. This is the administrative view, whereby, of course, the material, the technical nature of the pieces is considered. And here we want to raise the question: what about the adjustability of exchange rates?

In the last decades, until about the year 1890, the general belief was that exchange rates were destinies to which states must submit. The Minister of Finance read the bulletin in the morning with growing discomfort and went to his bureau annoyed when the exchange rate had fallen against his wishes. He thought, for instance, that an unfortunate economy is a pity that it must fall into my ministry; it would have been much nicer if this had happened to my predecessor. (Laughter.)

So here is the idea that one can not defend against the fluctuation of the exchange rate, even if one is finance minister. What do we see in recent times? Did not you realize that the Russian exchange rate, despite the Japanese war, which has truly been a bloodbath of the highest order for Russia, has been somewhat reduced since then, but has been comparatively less favorable to Russia? One hundred rubles - 216 Mk. - was the note on the Berlin Stock Exchange in 1903. Then came the unfortunate war for Russia, and now you can buy 100 rubles, not at 216, but at about 214 Mk. The difference is so compared to the year 1903 before the time of the Japanese war for the ruble 1%. Certainly very small.

And that's because the Russians have a regulation of their exchange rate and the man who does that, that is - Mendelssohn. (Laughter.) Mendelssohn in Berlin has two coffers, in one of which the rubles notes, in the other the Mark notes, and then he receives the order from the Russian Minister of Finance to exchange the ruble for 214 marks and the mark for as many kopecks. Thus, the fluctuation of the ruble exchange has simply disappeared, because the state jumped into the stock market fight and mediates as an overpowering fighter. Of course, from the point of view of the Minister of Finance, there is a very considerable moment involved: the Russians must increase their public debt in order to maintain this level of their ruble.

This costs the Russian state victims, but if the state wants to bring these sacrifices and can bring, then Mendelssohn can do his own and keep the exchange rate. So we see, the exchange rate can be kept in order, if there is a man who makes the corresponding sacrifices. For a well-ordered state that has not suffered such a disaster, as happened to Russia, the dangers are much lower, and it would be able to keep its exchange rate in order with fewer casualties. And in Austria? You know that the exchange rate in Austria with regard to Germany is of almost impeccable firmness. It's almost boring. The Austrian crown stands like a wall. There is nothing to speculate, that is a most benevolent phenomenon. If we inquire into the reasons for the firmness of this German-Austrian exchange rate, we see the explanation for this in the fact that the Austrian

Government and the Austrian General Administration, to which the Austro-Hungarian Bank belongs, have finally come to the conclusion that, if ordered Financial conditions, can keep this exchange rate at an almost absolute level through an orderly hand. Is this something of those writers who represent the metallic theory of monetary affairs? No. It does not belong there either; because that is administrative technology and not coin technology, that is the administrative activity of the state, and so he achieves this success. While the metallists can provide very nice information about the types of money, the administrative side of the question must now be taken into account, and it must be clearly understood that there are large institutions in our central banks that perform a dual function. First, because they are money-raising institutions - the shareholders want to see dividends - but then these institutions are also used by the state for certain purposes, which are in the field of regulatory change.

Of course, I completely admit that I have not been able to reasonably justify some of the sentences that I have said, but that is also impossible in the time available to me. Therefore I forbear those gentlemen who have to raise this or that objection in the spirit, for a little patience and forbearance. I just want to show where the whole thing is going, I want to express the conviction that if other scholars help us, we will soon have a sufficient theory of monetary administration to the side of the administration, then we will become the few, preserve and retell poor knowledge of coinage without putting this side of the question in the foreground.

As for state theory in relation to Austria, I can be very brief here. Austria has experienced terrible fates in relation to its constitution. The year 1811 is now almost a century past, the year 1848 brought an almost complete outgoing of cash in the state coffers, it came the forced course for the banknotes, the bonds came to the bank, she liked it or not; the state is right, and rightly so, because it has to maintain itself first of all, and for him a loan to the bank is a very subordinate matter, a minimum to the great tasks that the state as such has. This condition lasted until the Italian war, where Baron v. Bruck set up the monetary system on the basis of the silver currency, because Germany had the silver currency and not because he would have preferred silver.

This money constitution was destroyed, and when the damage was almost cured, the year 1866 came, and it had to be managed in Austria with state notes, in addition to the banknotes, until finally in 1892 the basis of the present monetary constitution was laid.

Austria is thus an empire which, although it has experienced very great misfortunes in the field of finance - certainly - and in particular the bar constitution has always avoided it. The forces were not enough. But this kingdom must be taken seriously.

One has to study it and have to ask: how the Austrians did it to get out of all these tribulations. Austria is the classic country - not for the best money in every moment - but where you can best study the monetary system and its development. How should we in Germany, which since the year 1876 has its present monetary constitution, how should we study the monetary system and its development on German material? Nothing has ever happened to this financial system. A monetary being, however, must be driven by fire and water in order to be tested. Destinies which hinder one another, calamities which oppress it, these are the conditions where money can best be studied. It is a false point of view to say that the Austrian constitution has seldom been normal for our scholars. This is especially for the study of the thing a preference. It was a misfortune for the state; but you can learn from it what interests us at the moment. Austria is precisely the country in which the development of the monetary system can best be studied because of the tremendous diversity of events. The state theory of money, which is currently emerging, is the theoretical expression of what has been experienced in Austria. To uniformly explain these experiences, the state theory of money is suitable for this purpose. We theorists do not give advance advice on what the bank president should do, what the finance minister and what the governor should do; Rather, we learn from those who are in life and seek to trace what has happened to the simplest of basic ideas. The Austrian state should not learn from us theoreticians, but we theoreticians first want to put into clear light what has happened, we want to shed the main point and leave aside the trivial. It seems like a modest performance. But in practical development, especially when things are very complicated, there are moments when the practitioner, in spite of his muddling and retreating, is very glad when once he is exposed to the simple train of thought of his actions.

This is the service which the theory of practice accomplishes because the practitioner lacks the time to eliminate the trivial with clear consciousness. The ordinary skipper knows nothing of nautical science, but he is grateful to the navigator if he gives him good advice. I am far from claiming the right to the theory to guide the practitioner on the path he has to go, but it is their job to illuminate the way the practitioners have traveled to open them up this way to facilitate the continuation of their journey. From this point of view, the state theory of money is to be judged. In the study of Austrian things, I have had the opportunity to become acquainted with a model

administrative law whose practical consequence and clarity can hardly be exceeded. The relation of state theory to Austria is that Austria has delivered the experiences that are presented in this theory.
(Great applause and clapping.)

Chairman Hofrat Professor v. Philippovich:
Professor Knapp, when he spoke again, would hardly say that he was in the minority. I believe he has already won a strong majority in this Assembly, and that will be our greatest thanks for his scientific endeavors and his presentation here.
(Applause.)

Eduard Hammer, a Viennese currency writer

Hammer has written and sent numerous small writings; I received two of them in the summer of 1893, together with a letter. At that time I was only beginning my studies of the Austro-Hungarian monetary system and knew nothing wrong with the brochures, so that I even forgot them. When, in 1905, I published the treatise on the State Theory of Money, I came with the Government Councilor Dr. Ing. Ludwig Calligaris, who informed me in August 1906 that a nerd named Hammer around 1892 had strongly advised the Austrian Government on the artificial regulation of exchange rates. Some of these writings were sent to me by Calligaris, a few others I owe to the efforts of the court and court advocate. Kuranda in Vienna. It was of great interest to hear the opinions of that nerd. Of his personal circumstances, very little was known.

In September 1906, I met a then 25-year-old gentleman from Vienna, Friedrich Gaertner, who promised me that he would fill the gap; He reported from Vienna on April 2, 1907:
Hammer, who was at last completely destitute, died in the general polyclinic, Vienna, IX., Mariannengasse 10, on January 28, 1906. The exact date of his birth was not known, it was only stated: "61 years old." He was born in Neubergruh in Prussian Silesia After further personal inspection of the files of that hospital, Mr. Gaertner added (April 23, 1907): Hammer was Protestant, Augsburg confessional, he died of liver cancer and was buried in the Vienna Central Cemetery on January 30, 1906. He had no permanent home or relatives, since there was no probate assets, and no probate act has been taken by the court.

On January 19, Dr. Kuranda enclosed a note to a booklet, which a colleague, whose name can not be deciphered, had sent to him; the colleague writes about Hammer:
All I know from him is that from 1872 to 1876 he was the chief accountant of the construction companies Wiener Bauverein, Stadtbaugesellschaft and Allgemeine Realitätengesellschaft, which represented three companies in a kind of cartel Bill, but did not come with a green branch, lived on a large foot until he had nothing left, then sank deeper and deeper, suffered as you know (Kuranda), in delusions of size and persecution, begged me and others often more not known.

Dr. Ignaz Gruber of the Austro-Hungarian Bank wrote to me (postmark 3 September 1906):
Hammer is well known to me. He visited me a lot at the Bureau about ten years ago ... His ideas sometimes had a good sense, but he was by the way not a very clear mind. In addition, he perished because he wanted his opinions immediately translated into practical terms. I believe that he was recently in financial embarrassment, as his hopes for realization of his currency projects failed.

Mr. Government Councilor Dr. L. Calligaris, also from the Austro-Hungarian Bank, wrote to me on January 23, 1907:
Even in his earlier days, Hammer made the picture of a completely shattered thinker, who never went to logical clarity. He only made correct statements; The reasoning was lacking, which obviously upset him, so he repeated himself and turned in circles, his face flushing feverishly and he could never finish. So he finally became a plague for those he visited again and again with his plans.

His sad material situation, in which he was probably not innocent, did not raise confidence.

After these very sad clarifications we take a look at the texts. They are all very short and leave the impression that the author can not completely master his cause. In addition to the small booklets that appeared in the book trade, he also had numerous quarto sheets printed, which he used to send, but Hammer takes up a position that is far removed from what was customary at the time: he sometimes counters that which one now Calling metallism; and he does not see salvation alone in the cash-on-banknotes. Unfortunately, the scriptures are written exactly as one would expect from the above descriptions of the person.

Some posts should be highlighted. Above all, Hammer has a clear idea of where the strength of the gold price comes from; At that time there were professors who thought that this strength was a characteristic of this metal!

We find in the writing: Eduard Hammer, "For the elimination of the Agios," Leipzig 1888, 47 pages, page 14 below:
"Today the silver is no longer bought by state administrations or exchanged for money silver coins, as a result also its price changes constantly; once gold is no longer bought by the states at fixed prices, or exchanged for gold ("money?"), the value of the gold will also change, that is dependent on demand and supply. "

On page 38 you will find the following remark under the text: *"Nowadays the price of gold is fixed by the fact that the States mentioned above buy every quantity of gold at a legally fixed price, for by obtaining gold there for every quantity of gold, this circumstance means that one can always deduce from the States can get a legally stipulated sum of money for a certain amount of gold, and that the state buys gold at fixed prices. However, this does not mean that the price of gold on the world market can easily change. "*

In another paper: Eduard Hammer, "The Main Principles of Monetary Policy", Vienna 1891, page 18, wrote:
"The price of gold, as well as that of all commodities, would be subject to change, depending on supply and demand, if its price were not fixed on the money market, that in many states the free coinage of gold coins takes place for the account of private persons For a given sum of money, you can always get the same amount of gold and vice versa for a given amount of gold you can always get the same amount of money. The price of silver is already, since the free form of silver for the account of private persons is set everywhere, as the price of each commodity, depending on supply and demand! "

The fact that Hammer was not a metalist (as we now say) can be seen from the following passage, which can be found in a printed page of four pages entitled "The program for the production of currency", dated: Vienna, den November 9, 1893, the passage reads:
"As a currency (or measure of value), however - as I have already stated in my various publications - functions and can only function, in our case, as in any other economy, a value unit accepted as a unit of value or statutorily fixed, such as the Guilder, the dollar, the rupee or similar, but never gold or silver. "

He summarized Hammers conception of the agio in Austria in a letter addressed to me from Vienna from 2 July 1893.
The letter shows a very clear commercial handwriting and was the answer to the fact that I wrote to him that I did not find his remarks on the agio in a brochure sent to me sufficient. He says:

"As regards your remark concerning the Agio and its origin, I allow myself to reply in the following. The agio, which is expressed in a price ratio of Austro-Hungarian money to the so-called gold money, which is suppressed by its pari, is a product of the gearbox on the money market, which settles on the stock exchanges. This transmission is today dominated by the following circumstances:
1. One holds money on the one hand and gold (formerly also silver) and foreign currency on the other hand for identical terms.
2. It is believed that silver or gold is the currency.
3. Identify the currency with the money.
4. It is understood that gulden, mark, rupee, or the like are "units of value" (not precious metals, coins, or even units of account), which constantly represent one and the same and absolute values, and finally
5. It is overlooked that a gulden coin or note, as long as it is fully accepted for a guilder, and thus the full payment power; d. i. per 1 guilder, always the same and absolute value, d. i. owns 1 guilder.

These circumstances are the cause of existence of Agio. As a result of these circumstances, the course of the so-called gold money has been pushed from its pari and suspended the exchange. By eliminating this cause, which can be obtained by means of the government measures proposed by me, the existence of an agios will become an impossibility. "

We add two more posts on the regulation of the value date. In the writing: "The measures for the establishment of definitively regulated value date conditions", Vienna 1894, it is called page 17:
"... It institutes must be created ... Such a institution is the exchange obligation, which is taken over immediately by the Austro-Hungarian bank and and by which everyone can obtain from this bank Austro-Hungarian money for foreign, such as German, French or English money, al pari shall be changed. "

Eduard Hammer opposes the cash payment; he writes in a printed sheet of four octave pages under the heading:
"Our agio and the management of our central bank", dated February 4, 1895:
"In view of the fact that the bank management was tied up in a chain of erroneous and outdated views concerning the nature of money, I have at the same time proved and informed the bank management: a) that the bank's view that one should be more definitive elimination of the agio required by the so-called "cash payments" was a mistake, b) etc. "

These are samples of places that are particularly clear. To give an excerpt that summarized Hammers system in a short while is not possible. In my opinion, the tragic case is that an unskilled person is made happy by single good ideas; he always tries to make it a whole, but it fails in every attempt. Nobody can deny him the merit of having wanted.

From Hammer's writings I have the following:

1. Basic principles for the Austrian economy. Vienna 1880; XXXII, u 54 p.
2, To eliminate the agio. Leipzig 1888; 47 pages.
3. The main principles of the monetary system and the solution of the valuta. Vienna 1891; 32 pages.
4. The production of Valuta, Berlin and Leipzig 1892; 27 pages.
5, To stabilize the new relation. Vienna 1893; 30 pages.
6. The measures to achieve definitive fair value ratios. Vienna 1894; 30 p. Of which a second verb. Aufl., Vienna 1894, also 30 p.
7. Principles for the Reform of Our State Life. Vienna 1895, in the publisher's publishing house; 34 pages.

Printed sheets, all in four-page format, are available to me:

a) The Vienna Stock Exchange; Vienna, 18 September 1888, 4 pages.
b) To solve the gold and currency question and to eliminate the Agios! 5 pages; Vienna, September 1889.
c) The program for the production of the valuta; 4 p. Vienna, 9 Nov. 1899.
d) To solve the valuta question; 3 pages. Vienna, May 8, 1894.
e) The reorganization of the Austro-Hungarian Bank; 7 pages. Vienna, April 27, 1894; in the self-publishing of the author.
f) Our premium and the management of our notes bank; 3 p. Vienna, 4 Feb. 1895.

www.ingramcontent.com/pod-product-compliance
Lightning Source LLC
Chambersburg PA
CBHW020444220526
45464CB00002B/857